POEM, HOME
AN ANTHOLOGY OF ARS POETICA

POEM, HOME

AN ANTHOLOGY OF ARS POETICA

Edited by
JENNIFER HILL
&
DAN WABER

© 2009 by Paper Kite Press
All rights reserved.

Printed in the United States of America
by BookMobile.

Cover art by David Hage (www.davidhage.com)
Cover design and page layout by Jennifer Hill

ISBN: 978-0-9798470-7-3

paper kite
press

Kingston, Pennsylvania
wordpainting.com

"A poem should not mean, but be."
— *Archibald MacLeish*

INTRODUCTION

Three years ago we had an idea: let's do an anthology of ars poetica — poems about poetry. We've both written poems about poetry, and figured most every poet has, too. Poets know other poets. They know poets with poems about poetry. We realized we knew not just poets with poems about poetry who know other poets with poems about poetry, but poets with poems about poetry who know other poets with poems about poetry who know still other poets with poems about poetry. Whew! And so began the whirlwind of words on poetry.

We built a blog and posted the first ars poetica. We then invited five other poets to send their ars poetica along with the names and email addresses of five other poets we could invite. One grew to five and that five grew to 125 and that 125 grew to 625 and so it exploded outward.

The invitation indicated that all poems submitted would appear on the website, and then, later, selections would be made for a print anthology — the print anthology that you now hold in your hands.

In the end, 803 poets were invited to submit their poems (362 additional names were provided but never invited because the response rate was so huge that the invitation process had to be shut down after only two months because we had over two years worth of poems to post). Five hundred and sixty-eight poems were submitted by 255 poets (a positive response rate of 3.14 for you math heads out there) and each was published to the website at logolalia.com/arspoetica at a rate of one per day. (We strongly encourage you to visit the website and view all of the poems submitted to this project.)

The posting of the poems to the website ended in January of 2009, and the selection process for this book began. This print anthology wasn't constructed to be a "Best Of" collection; it was constructed to lure you in to the project as a whole. There are many, many very fine poems which were submitted but do not appear here.

Whenever a collection such as this is put together the editors read not just for quality but also with a plan for the entire collection to hang together as a cohesive whole. We read each of these poems twice, in order to make our first "cut" based on yes/no/maybe. We then went back and read through them all again looking for the grouping whose sequencing would produce a collection that was as strong, taken as a whole, as any of the individual poems was, taken separately.

By making all of the poems submitted available for reading on the website, you also have the unique opportunity to oversee our choices, and our editorial vision. You have the ability to compare your choices with ours, and we hope you will take the time to do so, because it is a rich and rewarding experience to buoy through so many views through so many facets of the gemstone that is poetry.

We would like to thank Dawn Leas, Fran Hill, and David Hage for their help in putting this book together. We would also like to thank the poets involved in all aspects of the project, without whom none of this would be possible. We wish, lastly, to make special mention of those who were gracious, kind, and offered words of gratitude.

Enjoy!
Jennifer & Dan

TABLE OF CONTENTS

NOTES AND CREDITS

POEM, HOME

AN ANTHOLOGY OF ARS POETICA

KELLI RUSSELL AGODON

―――

You Ask Why I Write About Death and Poetry

There's *entirety* in *eternity*,
and in the *pearly gates* — the *pages relate*.

I fall *prey* to
            poetry,

have *hated*
            death.

You know, I've never understood *reality,*
        then try to *relay it* — *tearily, irately* —
        and I'm a *liar yet*.

But when I write about *death and poetry,*
        it's *donated therapy*
    where I converse with
    Emily Dickinson, my *inky misled icon*.

And when my *dream songs* are *demon's rags,*
        I dust my *manuscript* in a *manic spurt*
    hoping the *reader* will *reread*

because I want the world
to *pray for poets* as we are only *a story of paper*.

KELLI RUSSELL AGODON

———

Kindergarten for Poets

And it was at that age ... Poetry
arrived in search of me
— Pablo Neruda

Ignore Billy who's bothering Louise
with his sestina, repeating his six words
in her ear when he thinks the teacher
isn't watching:
dog,
    jazz,
        ghost, mouse,
angels, hat.

You're five and September is the month
of poetry subjects:
All About Me, Bones, Love, Roads, The Five Senses

Before your parents leave,
Mr. Pound says what you will do today:

Orally combine words to make a complete thought
Practice proper writing posture
The ABCs of reading

For show and tell, you bring in a cliché
and everyone points it out.

You write your first haiku:
in kindergarten
I still dream about being
in kindergarten

After story time, you tell the librarian
you enjoyed *Beowulf* just so he'll smile and nod.

Li-Young shares his peaches with you at lunch
and you want to touch his hand.

Back in class you realize you have a crush
on Sharon who keeps pulling up her dress.
Wallace mumbles something in the center
of circletime. Few can understand him,
but everyone smiles in agreement.

Quiet Jane prefers to sit alone with a fresh daisy
on her desk. She stares out the window
and notices how dandelions form
into letters: O, Q, lowercase i.
You share a desk with Gwendolyn
and listen to her stories.

In the days to come you will learn
there is no way to stop Logan
from kicking the back of your chair,
or reminding you
that you wore that shirt
yesterday, the same green shirt,
and you dot your i's wrong. In fact
everything you do is wrong. Well, not wrong,
but not necessarily right.
Later, Franz beats him up after school
and things feel better for a while.

On Halloween, you dress up like a pantoum
and repeat yourself all day.

You are starting to believe
couplets are for babies.

For Valentine's Day, you write,
I want to eat your skin like a whole almond
on your cards, and the principal
calls you into her office
to ask you if you're getting enough
to eat at snack time.

Sometimes you forget and run with sestinas.

Next year, you'll begin first grade
and will be introduced to book contests,
submissions, and rejections.

Now, your poems are returned
with smiley faces, stickers, and stars.

You're happy in this iambic universe,
this phonic jungle where the alphabet
wraps around the room —

Jack-Jack Kerouac, ă, ă, ă.

You wear your sonnet like a cape
and revise the words that spill
from your backpack —
verbs hang from the monkey bars,
nouns lean against the bike rack,
a villanelle of mockingbirds echo
as the bus comes into view.

FLOR AGUILERA GARCIA

The Fair

Outside Mont Royal station there is a market.

Rimes are sold, verses exchanged,
dissonances repaired and sonnets modernized.

A woman approaches, in want of inspiration.

This is all I have, she says to the poet-salesman,
her hand extended.

For that amount, he answers
you can buy one word.

She chooses randomly,
Twilight appears.

They congratulate her purchase.
It's a very poetic word, they all say,
a key that will open many doors.

The woman returns home, saddened,
she feels her way in the darkness, turns on the light.

She does not want to open doors,
but to shut them hard.

She does not want to make poetry for those
who climb and fill the skies each morning, their
wide open hands and shiny, clean hearts;
but for those who are just
learning to crawl
on the soiled streets
their eyes alert.

KARREN LaLONDE ALENIER

Stein Writes It All Down

On our way
not knowing
where we go
Poof! The past
gone. Abra ca
dab the door
to tomorrow still
shut as we stand
watching the hands
of the grandfather tick
tock. I say: delete
commas. Period!
Repeat for the daily
dilly demands
attention.

SANDRA ALLAND

———

SASE

(a composite poem of complete sentences from Rampike,
Zygote, Black Cat 115, ink, Cencrastus, Broken Pencil, above/
ground press, Coach House Books, Brick, Blood &
Aphorisms, pedlar press, Quarry Magazine, Descant, and
The New Quarterly)

Dear Ms. Alland,

You'll notice this is neither
an acceptance nor rejection letter.
There is no logical reason
for this decision.
Recently we rejected work
from a writer who won
the $5000 Stephen Leacock Award
two weeks later. Actually,
this might mean it is better
to be rejected by us
if you want to become
rich and famous.

Because our magazine
is created in the scraps
and odd shavings of time
between paying our rents
and living our lives,
choosing work for each issue
is a painful experience.
We prefer works
that display polyphonic
and dialogical qualities.
This prevents us from taking
some exceptionally fine writing.

Competition was fierce.
Many projects were meritorious.
As you can imagine, the majority
of submissions come from writers
we either publish
or who are friends of the magazine
in some way.

Unfortunately however. Please see
the list below for reason(s)
we could not use your work
this time. You should hear from us
in January.
I apologize for the time it has taken.
Whatever though do keep in touch.
Please consider becoming
a subscriber.

We would have encouraged you
to try again, but, unfortunately,
we are ceasing publication.

Writing is an occupation which,
generally speaking,
requires a great deal of solitude.

It has become necessary
to make use of these terribly
impersonal reply slips.
We have all received
these letters and cursed
the fools who sent them.
We hope you understand.
You definitely have potential.

Sincerely,
The Editor

P.S. I think I'm in the next
Paperplates too. If it ever comes out ...
I'm reading at the Imperial Pub
next week. See you there?

Lost While Translating

There's this woman I'm reading.
No, that's not right.
There's a woman —
open like a book.
Still not it.
Her heart an ancient text.
My heart the devouring eyes.
No.

There's a woman,
she has words like no one,
sentences like never,
a woman I lost like a train
for a faraway land.
Not what I mean.

In English, you say,
What are you reading?
Rarely who.

There was a woman,
and I kept reading
what I'd been reading before.

C. J. ALLEN

The News and the Weather

Too much has already been said

about the spring. More than enough
ink has been squandered on the fall.

It would be impossible to entirely cast out
the volumes that dwell on light.
That winter is marching steadily

down from the hills is as much
yesterday's news as ripples of sand
on the beach being like something
or something else. The wet-linen

colour of almost every cloud
in literature is, frankly, boring.
It is time to address other things:
empty boxes of rain that are sometimes
trees, the neglected battalions of grass ...

C. J. ALLEN

————

The Duck's Back and How
it Got Like That

You have taken to returning
to the old notebooks,
where the other life is,
'the properly narrated one',
where you consider the duck's back
and how it got like that,
the morphology of clouds,
how stars explode, the habits
of gravity and time. These days
you wake up in the dark

and ask yourself what you know:
the names of the Telemark saboteurs;
how the best way of writing about it
is never writing about it; that the light
at the end of the tunnel is no chink
in the gloved and greaved murk
of Erebus, neither is it the apocryphal
oncoming locomotive. It is only
some bastard with a torch.
He is not looking for you.

C. J. Allen

Poetry is Your Friend

It's undeniably true, life
weathers you. There's no doubt
about that. Gardens crammed
with slightly creepy little elves,
a van parked on a deserted lane,
the sky almost purple when you look out.

That's when you turn to poetry.
You may not know it of course,
but that's what you'll be doing.
You're doing it right now, superficially
despite yourself, riding this wave
of energy out of nowhere. It feels good,

doesn't it? Like a high-sugar drink
or that special moment, you know
the one. It's here to help
even if it sometimes forgets,
gets all wrapped up
in counting syllables and such.

It wants you like a tyrant or the sun.

IVAN ARGUELLES

[ars poetica]

angry that, Bernice's lock
doth no one show, who think
that to "get it off your chest"
is all, meaning of, sitting
for hours for the noonday
class the wine growing tepid
the oblong shadow, of doubt,
of fear and the Man, over how
many days the epic struggles
first in hashed latin then
in obbligato cinquecento prose
finally as an after struck to
the unsounded chord, the rampant
shield aloft sun's glint the
Eye doth dart, hovering behind
clauses of rejection, pink stray
pages can go nowhere, isn't that
what? essentially at war with
syntax, with the elemental
emotion, ghosts, who rhyme
with darkness pleasure's ancient
ore, is it the peacocks in tumult
for rage and scorn alike?
is it for Mnemosyne the muse
of pearl-green hue?
is it for the variegated bloom
that adorns the suffix fair?
for whom is this catastrophe
of orange-red dust and powders?
is it heaven-sent we come to flail
among thunderstone and cliff?
+++++++++++++++++++++++++++++++
who come to study not life
but its mundane chores and charnel
house the whores delectable a
prize in midden-heaps for those
that counting is the only game
for those who cannot above prose
rise, is it not hell their one

and only fane the boulevards
of littered prosody, come then
away to groves and shrines
where mystery, to dreams that
through cloud scrapes break!
here, admit "I do not understand"
+ +
is it to purple luster bruise
the Ear in sweet remorse doth tend?
how then does the assassin sing?
whence these Harpies to whom Meat
doth cling? Ah No more
quod I in shrouded verse aspire
the elysian fields to espy
the dire moly and asphodel to eat
isn't that what warned us once
to remove from sight th'Infernal
and in meadows bleak to ply
the unsown shadows of dead the
angels who in Hell conspire
+ +
who will no more come summer's
plush to enjoy nor lake and mere
beside what slight waves in breeze
ruffled move in some small sleep
who dreaming in choirs vast
of languages radiant and beyond
gyres that tumbling round the
shafts of darker planet's score
warriors cleft from the Lamp
face down in miasmic gore, did
this one remember ever May's
bright? in hospitals gather
by bedside verse and to archaic
statues implore what Grief!
+ +
is it to love the flower the many-
sided in winds swaying how sweet
remembrances in azure crystallize
and die
"remember Me" doth Narcissus
slake his breath in depthless Pool

doth Hyacinth then lament
upon his shepherd's rock
the day-long grass of tears
and rent his cloak in briars
running like one Mad
into the fierce Unknown
is it to love then, Heart?
how words woven take on their own
subsiding never,
+++++++++++++++++++++++++++++++
now recline and die Thy little death
it is to Love, was once by might
taken suspended High above
while in the foaming spent of eons
the years unnumbered went
+++++++++++++++++++++++++++++++
"doth ever Rose so swoon and pale?"

—————

Ars poetica

A spree of poets brings lustful joy
jets roses on the coastal approach
from Creole land to highest peaks
from papaya's golden warmth
to alpaca's dream
or distant relics through windy fifes
"sacred urns" to visions of more human souls

jot down notes
on a white screen
inside scream
the burning fire
of dual lives, the Tao:
the black and the white
from the pit to a ray
from the Plutonic mine
to the careful lip
pleas in the court
to escape apes (sorry my apes read through the
lines)
kind elves to appease thirst
floating on the sea of lies
like a freezing floe
the small isle of Ars Poetica
the one of Ars
the soil of Ithaca
in the eyes of a father
a suffering mother

and type and joke
like a cheerful foal
play the apocalypse
when on the threshold it destroys
pray the saints
as if they were

Saint Thomas Merton
Saint Ezra Pound
Saint Frederick Nietzsche
Saint Charles Baudelaire
Saint Arthur Rimbaud
Saint Jorge Luis Borges
Saint Jack Kerouac
Saint Jeff Harrison
Saint Chris Murray
Saint James Finnegan
Saint Tad Richards
Saint Bill Lavender
Saint Joel Weishaus
Saint Tom Beckett
Saint Jean Okir
Saint Adam Fieled
Saint Michael Rothenberg
Saint Mike Peverett
Saint Joseph Duemer
Saint Karl Young
Saint Mary de Rachewiltz
Saint Paolo Ruffilli
Saint Eileen Tabios
Saint Nives Simonetti
Saint ...

Saint Atop
Saint teasers
Saint potato eaters
Saint flowers
Saint peseta
Saint spies
Saint toys
Saint Niece
Saint root, fir, jet, riff, rye, yes, five and six, paper,
air, poesy, toffee, pet, jar, palace, ore, year, leaf,
offer, frost, role, loser, jasper, obsidian, seal, piffle,
foray, pier, jester, self, lore, polar bears, opals, lap,
portals, twelve, salty oars, trees, life, portraits,
flipping pole, people

Poets

GARY BARWIN

The Chest Hairs of Language, Dear Reader

My writing is a needle shortening the pants of
        monotony and dread
It leaves an impressive thread as it winds through
the abbreviated cuffs of you who hitherto did
        proceed trippingly through the daily
        darkness and stumble of everyday speech

My writing rides a bicycle through the stitchholes
        of your hems
the fabric of your mind stretched by my thousand-
        speed cosmic roadbike cosmos with
        wheels of pure joy
and your thoughts
undiscovered planets embraced by a multitude of
        imperceptible moons
suddenly are Hubble-ized and named by the per-
        spicacious cartographic lexicon of my
        cerebral sewing

For I am a one-handed phrenologist kneeling in a
        haberdasher's fantasyworld funhouse,
a contestant playing the carbon dating game with
        the moon-fearing bachelorettes of my
        ancestors

Through the chest hairs of language, my poems
        seek gold medallions and the burnished
        signs of the zodiac in the mythic
        resonance of the curly pectoral forest
my writing is a BeeGee sestina Hallelujah Chorus
a John Travolta post-structuralist jumpsuit
        fandango of literary theory
a Hilary Duff post-colonial mega-sized writing
        samba in the blog roll drive-thru

My poetry contains multitudes and they appear
      small within its vastness
a single molecule within the molehill of my talent
I write on a desert island and the desert island feels
      glad
signals the boats of meaning, the search-and-rescue
      helicopter critics
says, stay away
stay away for we have something here

Yes, I'm a bachelor married to the archipelago of my
      own poetry
going on a date with me would be like Y2K all over
      again
an excitement of digits, an anticipation of
      irrational calculations, airliners seeking the
      arcing chaos of their own inspirational
      routes through the cloud-busy air
a date with me would be like changing from the
      Gregorian to the Julian Calendar while
      hang-gliding through the National
      Library dressed in an asbestos nightie
      while the books are inflamed
the librarians run blindly down the stacks and
      inhale the smoking grammar of our lives
headbutting the opposing players of tedium,
      madness, and apathy as they attempt to fan
      the bookish flames with facile rhymes,
      trite metaphors, and a limited
      understanding of the depth of my literary
      consciousness

I am the book-wheezy Jeffersons of this last
      century, the poetic Archie Bunker of our times
I speak of Love Connection glory
of radiant Gilligan's Island subplots singing
Partridge Family small press bliss in the
      triumphant World Cup publishing paradise of
      Toronto
A date with me would be like having God's credit card,
      Satan's expense account, and the
      incisive ontological wardrobe of Samuel
      Beckett if he were born as one of the

midget stagecrew for Gladys Knight and the
Pips and his daddy owned the big
rhinestone factory on the outskirts of sense.

Look! Someone's revved the motor, turned on the
highbeams of language's monster
truck
Seems like its blind driver has floored it and is
driving to you a first date
it's 1849 and it's with me

GARY BARWIN

Beautiful Dog

the field beside my heart is
filled with ugly deer and one beautiful dog

a poem doesn't have to have 14 perfect lines
or else you're spitting on graves

maybe you'll slip up and tell a truth
stick your flaking elbow into something rich

under the moon your tongue hangs out
you'd like to howl but there's this language thing

the pile of shame grows and grows
please save my family from complication or sudden death

listen: a small movement in the linden leaves
the poem collapses small and leaping

be brave be brave be brave

the field beside my heart is
filled with ugly deer and one beautiful dog

and here's another beautiful dog
sighing sighing sighing

L

No poems for three months, no near poems,
I revise, clean up, throw out. I index the survivors
by first word or key word. No X or Z, of course,
but at least one poem for every other letter —
except L. And how can that be? The one who loves her
        family,
loves her friends, loves her lovely garden,
loved the lovers who long ago moved on,
has nothing left to say?

What about Laughter? What about Life?
Am I waiting to be named queen of Loss
and Loneliness?
Better to settle for lunch
in the small French restaurant downtown
where a casual companion
lifts my hand to his lips whispering, *La langue,*
time now to speak of light verse.

RICK BENJAMIN

Growing Up

One part's abstract — listening
to an underground river clearing
its throat in the desert & thinking
about the Yucca tapping their roots

down to those drops — &
the other part's a scene
from a movie: waking up
to a pale moon in half-

morning light feeling the tip
of a knife at your throat, and
just before hearing him say,
there's a scorpion on your neck;
I'm going to flick it into

the fire thinking *I guess*
this is it, he's finally going
to do it. On one side
of this is hearing the sharp

sizzle of a scorpion
in flames; on the other
is the rest
of your life.

Two Arts

My old last name
nearly rhymed
with *taxidermy.*

Rhymes with "attorney"
my mother would say
to anyone who asked how
to pronounce it.

& If my sister's life
had been hers
to draw up
she'd be a lawyer

today, not just someone
who meditated for twenty
years in the middle
of a forest never making

a name for herself. *She should
have used her head for something else
besides a hair garden,* mother says.

My sister's name still rhymes
with *attorney.* If you take out
the "t" in the word *poverty*
and put an "n" in its place

that's how you spell it.
It's not that hard
to change your name.
You fill out some forms

& they put an ad in the paper
in case you're changing it
for the wrong reasons.
The rest is like blowing

air through a pipe & making
a glass bubble.
Or that other art,

bringing back to nearly
life some dead form,
performing *that* act
of animation.

JOHN M. BENNETT

Art of Poetry

I sat before the shattered screen the
wire plugged in and ground my teeth the
splintered bone was words to calculate
the random breakage pattern of the glass;
the words took shape, became 3D, grayish
worms that slicked the jagged points, a
crown of buns, a heart with twisting bacon at the
center, crossed buzzsaws rising to the sky

MAXIANNE BERGER

The Other Woman's Poem

I found another woman's poem under the pillow
on your side of the bed. Your taste in literature
appears to be improving, but I analyzed
her craft, found schemes in her motif.
The meter moving my stanzas, active with
your verbs, takes its rest in the everyday
language of your arms. Her lines are contrived
to simulate excitement, drawing on shades
of forbidden form.
                    Yet after a few readings
you'll crumple it in boredom, discard it
like so many others before. Philologaster,
I realize that no wife can keep you
from burrowing your wormy way through
other women's verse, but don't naively hide
the folded facts under your pillow:
remember who changes the sheets.

F. J. BERGMANN

How to Write Poems # 510

Spelling is very important.
She was excited about
the bottle of gin, but
disappointed when
what came out of it
wouldn't grant
any wishes at all

F. J. B<small>ERGMANN</small>

How to Write Poems # 86

See, you take a language
you don't even know
and make up whatever
you think it looks like
it could say. *Schickelgruber*
becomes "shackled grubs"
or "sickle groove." Or "chick
leg rubber." Words are
squirming Rorschach splats
and you have a condition
not described in the DMS-IV.
Pictograms and hieroglyphs
are more, or possibly less,
accommodating. Barcodes are
the most challenging.

F. J. Bergmann

How to Write Poems # 49

Rip a page from a defective
dictionary, or a dull novel. Cross
out the words you don't need,
like *unnecessary* or *egregious*;
words you don't like, such as
homeland or *atrocity*; words you
don't want, like *heart* or *knife*.
You may be left with nothing
but articles or pronouns,
those monosyllabic grunts
indicative of something
like passion, or pain.

CLIFF BERNIER

Baja

Pitaya & cholla in the Sierra de Juárez
landscape the ridge of the Rio San Miguel
the desert reversing the sea
the communion of tamarind & cinnamon
on the tongues of arroyos
naming the townships Bajamar, La Salina, Punta Morro
after the sign of the surf

& voice the scroll of the tide in the blue fan palms
& the bleached shells of crabs on the black stone beach

In the orchard of Santo Tomás
a laborer
heart bruised like a peach
gathers the fruit
the grapes bunched like a rosary
the pears wicked like candles
the sacrament of orange & wheat
in the grove
by the ruins of the mission
& reads in the leaves
of the valley
the book of his faith
yucca mesquite cirio agave
the salt vowels of the breeze
& the text of his litany
on the flecked sea

Under the plums of the moon
I am the laborer
by the wide strokes of the waves
I harvest these lines
the print of the gull & the piper
the ribbon of fig on the mesa
the ray of the brittle-star
brilliant as grace
my hoe is the stalk of a pen
my tablet the pages of corn

my rows are the swells of the Bahía Descansos
Bahía de Todos Santos
the mass of the dry scrub of Baja
the field of the provident sea

GREGORY BETTS

———

ars poetica: the language of light verse

upon reading w. h. auden

A
candle
amplifi
er in
an
empty
room   leaves   shadows,
initiates   gaps,   a   darkness
lurks   in   corners.   Put   a
mirror,   fitting   strangely,   put
up   a   clue   strangely,
strangely   clustered   glass,
piling up optic until all sides
blaze,   the   one   inch   flame
now a huge deviant light: the
pacific   room   shines   in   the
illusion of blaze. By just a
candle, inhibit the chaos sea.
Each glass echo is a word,
illuminates   off   shadow.
Alive, this author room, this
fun   biopic   indication   of
space,   of   spacing,   of   the
celestial   geometry   of   light
disseminates,   rebounding
endless   echoes,   grows   to
depict heat until there is no
room   left,   no   beatific
candles,   no   walls.   Left   is   a
fragment   of   the   holder's
glass,   still   burning,   long
after   the   spilt   wax   has
disappeared   into   the   cold.

CELIA BLAND

Ars Geologica

Don't plumb it. Stones
don't allow uniformity
of line, although
some will break off outcroppings, digressive
noses with their hammers
but that's a sin against
stones. Concentrate on fitting one
rock striated with quartz or hardened
lava into a rock
veined with pyrite, that almost-gold.
Then do it again with granite.
No mortar. Each rock must bear
the weight and share
the weight in three dimensions.
How high? Let the stones
have their say. Here,
put your ear to the wall.
Nothing? You must hear
the enjambment: stone
stONE, STONE, STone, stone.

DEAN BLEHERT

Private Eye

He was nervous — they always are,
the new ideas, fidgeting in front of
my big desk. I didn't have to ask
what he wanted. I'd seen it all before:
The threadbare concept, the vague, tired image,
bathed in unearthly light. "Look," I said,
"Why don't you go to the press?
They can find words for anything,
fast and cheap." "You don't understand —
I'm a very private thought. You
are a private poet, aren't you?"
"You bet." (Three cob-webbed file cabinets full
of private poetry.) "But I don't handle
love poems. They're nothing but
trouble. Make a bum out of you
every time." I cracked my knuckles.
His cigarette ashes missed the tray.
"But you're my last hope! I've tried
greeting card writers, novelists, cartoonists —
I even begged a whole English Lit. and
American Studies Department! No one
would help me. I simply must have a
Poet!" His eyes were as bloodshot
and chaotic as my own. But what
the hell, I'd had nothing else to
say lately, and there was a strangled
eloquence about him, just the hint of
a new angle. If I'd known then
where it would lead me — tangling
with six rough drafts, getting tied up
in a sestina, fighting off a mob
of sentiments, the blood-chilling message
from Mr. Big (" ... indeed sorry ... cannot use
your work ... "), and most of all HER, Muse, sweet, sad
Muse, those big dumb eyes pleading
with mine to go on, find the missing words
somehow — Ah, Muse, what did I
get you into! ... Had I known, I wonder, would I

still have returned his feverish stare
(He had to be expressed, see —
it takes some of them that way) and
said so nonchalantly "Okey dokey, I'll give it
a whirl ..."

DEAN BLEHERT

Thirst

The things one is afraid to say
are also the things everyone else
is afraid to say. Ten people lean
on a bar, chatting and drinking,
each rough-edged fragments of themselves,
howling coyote souls under sedation,

yet to themselves and each other
as complete as any rock or chair.

When the anesthetic wears off
suddenly, alone in a room
full of gesticulating furniture,
one knows an agony no rock could bear.

Then, to release from stone faces
a trickle to quench desperate thirst,
one strikes terrible blows
that destroy mere flesh.

I too am parched, but I am commanded
only to speak to the rock. It will —
knowing then what can be said —
give forth water.

DEAN BLEHERT

How Poetry is Done

You can make any sentence poetical
by mentioning blood or bone.
For example, instead of "Yesterday
I went to the store," say "Yesterday
I went to the blood and bone store."
Instead of "The moon rose", say
"The blood moon rose" or "A bone
of moon rose" or, best, "A bone
of blood moon rose". For "I love you"
try "Bone and blood I love you".
Bone and blood are instant intense.
For profound, add in an inapplicable
abstraction, such as "geometry" or
"calculus", or a scientific reference
like "hologram" or "ecology", and
throw in a juicy verb. For example,
"The geometry of blood laments
this hologram of bone". But intense
and profound are not enough. You need
an ironic (hip) sense of mortality, as in "Chanting
its inevitable theorems in every fatty cell,
the geometry of blood laments this
fading hologram of bone" except that
"theorems" makes too much sense
with "geometry", so change "theorems"
to "charade" (not "singsong", which
makes too much sense with "chanting").
This gives us a satisfactory
Twentieth Century poem written
in a fresh unique authoritative etc. voice,
especially if the line lengths
are a bit weird, for example:

Chanting
its inevitable charade
in every fatty cell
the geometry of blood
laments this fading
hologram of
bone

Entitle it Collage #7 and send it
right out to a very little magazine
or anything that ends in "REVIEW".

poems

it's funny
we speak
nod our heads
and smile
but our only form of conversation is through poems
words that weave and float and fly

deciphering is required
but often there's no time —
there are buses to catch
movies to watch
drinks to drink
and the house needs a good spring cleaning

I hear the poems
but how will I know if I've understood your metaphors
and you, mine?

when I say
I walked into the room

what part will you understand?

when you say
my breath disappears from view

what will it mean to me?

PETER BOYLE

*In response to a critic's call
for tighter editing*

A poet should be able to write outside of the human in all sorts of
directions. The moon is one of them. Water that has just bubbled
out of the earth is another. Of course they are distant cousins as
intimately related as the wind and a sandgrain.

If I was the moon I couldn't practise what I would say. I would have
to be empty and desolate. Everything would happen by instinct like
tides responding to my slow ballet. I would be ignorant as a worn
shoe condemned to dance forever over subterranean waters. My
cratered eyes would guide me through space and my children would
say, *Look, he comes from forever, he's on his way to forever. He's
the one blind man whose walking stick is the glide of small fish
over sand, the waterfall that flows simultaneously in both directions.*

Of poetry

Great poems are often extraordinarily simple.
They carry their openness
with both hands.
If there is a metaphor lounging in a doorway
they step briskly past.
The boom of generals
and presidents with their rhetoric manuals
will go on sowing the wind.

The great poems are distrustful of speech.
Quietly,
like someone very old
who has only a few hours left of human time,
they gaze into the faces around them —
one by one

they kiss love into our mouths.

Medicine Tree

A disbeliever down to the bone,
he kneels before the stunted tree
alone in the feverish desert

called sleep. Various offerings —
wells of ink, plaster statuettes,
pages yellowed by time and heat —

from those who, like him,
once hoped to be forgiven or healed
lie scattered around. No doubt

he desires the persimmon
seeds, some kind of constellation
to give mercy, mercy enough.

Such windfallen fruit.
Such impossible sweetness.
Nothing here, says coyote.

Don't listen, says man. *Believe.*
When enough is spent, the sainted
tree seems to creak, seems to whisper,

on words reverently pronounced
as ritualistic appeasements,
only then will the buffalo's head

propped here in the highest fork
listen and reply. A spoonful of maggots
swims in each ear and the slack mouth.

The man snatches lines from the wind,
uproots them along with the pale grass
and swallows alkali. Nothing.

He praises the wind's countless
moods, that grass for its democracy.
Nothing at all. He strikes flint

for illumination and misses the mark,
drawing blood. One eye in the head opens
halfway. The wound is not enough.

Tonight the first poem will happen.

Revision

The story reinvents itself
each night around the campfire.
Once in Ireland, for example,
upon a time some terrible storm
left a horse high up in a tree

or if someone lives by the sea,
then a seal. In the highlands,
a goat stands in, regardless
of what each has in common:
always a figure which has lost

its position in the appropriate world,
erased by chance or embellishment.
And when the wind blows through
the treetops, a baby and cradle will fall
out of one version and into another.

This tree could burst into flames
at any moment or be felled by an ax
wishing to carve more of its kind.
The story, though, goes on and on,
unafraid, untouched but changed.

Ars Poetica

In the Indian museum
even the smallest basket
woven for just one bean
is banded red.

Why Poetry

Consider how
in a picture of a breast
taken by smashing the tissue
onto cold, marked glass
and shooting it through
(take a small breath and hold)
with penetrating poison light —
may be found something significant.

Working Method

fragments from:
"Ana Buigues' Selected Wrytings 2002-2005"
http://noemata.net/ab/
http://noemata.anart.no/ab/
ISBN 978-82-92428-48-1
ISBN-10 82-92428-48-8
Net.books: støttet av Norsk Kulturråd - supported by Arts Council
Norway

Date: Tue, 1 Nov 2005 18:16:03 -0000
Sender: "WRYTING-L : Writing and Theory across Disciplines"

From: Ana Buigues
Subject: working method

1.write it down

2.email it

Date: Tue, 1 Nov 2005 18:19:57 -0000
Sender: "WRYTING-L : Writing and Theory across Disciplines"

From: Ana Buigues
Subject: working method

1.inspiration sometimes comes when cleaning email that has been
piling up in
my inbox for the last year

2.reading outdated emails, calls for papers that i missed, letters
from nice
people that i couldn't even answer, kiss off letters i received in
response
to some job applications, and drafts i started and never finished,

makes
one realize that time flies.

3.this apparently mindless task becomes a triggering point for deep
reflection, and reconsideration of one's life and work.

In the room where I never wrote

there is a window, a mile view
of a beach I never walked
and sea stacks corkscrewing
up through surf I never heard
breaking

In the room where I never wrote
there is an oval wood table
piled with poems I never wrote
about desert sky,
eros,
and leaving my son

In the room where I never wrote
on that same table sits
the canyon book
that never sings
of my year in the hills,
the apple orchard,
cows trampling the spring,
lynx on the road,
yellow columbine

In the room where I never wrote
there are poems
that never speak
of a tent by Pacific volcanoes,
by the Stillaguamish River
with *Magister Ludi* in my hand
and no money

In the room where I never wrote
fall is eternal and its long light
fills the room gold,
and the keyboard sings,

from hands that never tire
molding poems stolen
from the dead, gifted
from the living

Donald Hall would hate me

if he knew me
I don't want to be great

it takes me 10 minutes
to write a poem

sometimes
& then

I want to whisper or
shout it about
town

my poems are *usually brief*
they *resemble each other*
they *are anecdotal*
they *do not extend themselves*
they *make no great claims*
they *connect small things to other small things*

I LIKE SHORT!

I just want to kick the leaves
& have done

NICK CARBÓ

For My Friend Who Complains
He Can't Dance and Has a Severe Case
of Writer's Block

Then, take this tambourine
inside the sheep barn,

listen to the anaconda's intestines,
the shark's walking stick,

learn the river insect's secret
neon calligraphy,

swim through Frida Khalo's hair
and come out smelling like orchids,

lift your appetite
towards the certified blue turtle,

feast on Garcia Lorca's leather shoes
and taste the sun, the worms of Andalusia,

don't hesitate in front of a donut,
a ferris wheel, the crab nebula,

excavate diamond-eyed demons,
Chaucer's liver, Minoan helmets,

paste Anne Sexton's face on a $1,000 bill
and purchase a dozen metaphors,

beware of the absolute scorpion,
the iguana with the limping leg,

permit indwelling, white words around the eyes,
the confrontation of windows,

never feed your towel to the alligator,
he will eat you and eat you and eat you.

Firing Squad Or Peanut Butter

They're just words, after all,
ink pressed into pulp,
or air spat from split lips.
So why concern yourself
with cunt or radish, their difference —
consonants, vowels.
Tricycle or grenade, does it matter
which word a child plays with?
Rape, lump, castrate, flay,
lynch, malignant, gouge, extinct —
harmless as slugs
or as nuclear fission.

WENDY TAYLOR CARLISLE

The Poem Avoids
the 'Sincerest Style'

When the poem comes to say what it knows about the
suprasternal notch, it stops. The pale hairs curling back against
the skin are far too personal a detail to render. The poem vowed
months ago never to speak of its erotic life again. Today's suitable
topics do not include the weight of flesh in the palm. The poem
shuns also the plane tree and fig for surely alluring fruit poisons
the page where a fir can never whisper nor willow weep again. But
what of the moon, the breast-pink oleander and lupine the color of
the edge of daylight — all of nature lit from within like a de la Tour
painting?

The poem shrugs and shuffles away from the lake and the ginger
daylilies, the pelt of moss on a park bench. It can only surrepti-
tiously admire a hip, an elbow but must eschew the eyes as too
close to tears, too skewed to the heartfelt which the poem has to
admit it can no longer abide. A reader might imagine the poem
looks better with its clothes off but that is another poem altogether
and one that concerns itself with sweat that can only be alluded
to here, where the poem attends to its cartoon nature and, dressed
like Doris Day, waits for a plane, reapplies mascara and adds to its
list of unsuitable topics which include the Alps, restaurants with
linen table cloths and all of Italy. The poem must also drive away
from metaphor which grows smaller and smaller in its rearview
mirror.

Thirty years ago a poem could lie in bed all day moaning heart!
heart! And then break. Today, the moon-free poem has no
vernacular for longing. It is a dream of itself in which a lover, if he
arrives, comes too late.

James Cervantes

In Lieu of an Ars Poetica

I've cut the string. The kite levitates. It hangs right in there at 2 o'clock, its red vibrant against the blue sky.

The birch bends beneath it. We are all in the wind and my link with the kite is strong. I can't bear to look down. My body feels the gusts and I become very aware of my ribs. The kite is motionless but I sense its minute pulse, its love with the wind.

Sal, my neighbor, comes out in the late afternoon and feels the air around me. No strings, Sal. No fishline, no radio-control. The damned kite just hangs there.

Almost evening, the sky a cobalt blue and the red kite with a halo. Sal has binoculars and is examining the kite for ailerons.

Let Sal demonstrate wonder: I am as buoyant as the kite. There's the bodiless voice of my neighbor, and myself, an ethereal witness, totally satisfied, thankful I have no hands to caress the kite.

Sal says I have a martini in my hand. Thanks, Sal. I lift it without looking at it, feel a tingle at my lips, then with one hearty gulp toast the kite. The feeling is impossible, like an ice cube floating in air.

It is evening and only I can see the kite, that diamond shape where there are no stars. In the morning there are no stars, and no kite. But there is space for another.

JOEL CHACE

―――

no matter

is this right then   we put

all our ducks in a row   all

our ducks of the under-word   all made

of quarks   which are or are

not matter but certainly are not

meaning   though the ducks

mean   as we line

the ducks up they make

a surface   a surface of

water   surface and water that

are not do not matter but

do mean   the matter then

cannot mean   the meaning is

nothing   but we keep

on lining up the ducks   beneath

the surface of water

is depth the more ducks the more

depth   and dark   and

murk   all of which is no

matter   no matter   not matter   but is

dark murk and deep   story

layered upon story   stories without

matter but with meaning   how

is it possible to live like

this   to make stories that

mean   but are no matter

JOEL CHACE

wedding

the word to the cave

no part of the space that is not

the word   the cave after

all is the space   the word after all

others is all the space that

is the cave

ELLEN ARONOFSKY COLE

Chimeric Poetica

*"A Stanford University researcher has gotten a preliminary go-
ahead to create a mouse with a significant number of human
brain cells – as long as the creature behaves like a mouse, not
a human."*
- *MercuryNews.com*

Mouse-brain with human cells writes poetry.
Mouse-body scratches on her nubbled cage floor
verses praising the intricate structure of cheese.

Random spheres in yellow flesh, unseen
and empty, spark delectable reflection.
Mouse-brain with human cells writes poetry.

Scientist gnaws on pencils, concludes, fleas.
His mono-species brain fails to receive
verses praising the intricate structure of cheese.

Alert for human traits, he does not see
what rodentia plus homo sapiens achieves;
mouse-brain with human cells writes poetry.

Mouse-brain with human cells begins to grieve.
Distraught, she darts about her cage, destroys
verses praising the intricate structure of cheese.

Disregarded, Mouse-brain falls into depression.
Apathetic, slow, writes Scientist, unknowing.
Mouse-brain with human cells wrote poetry
praising the intricate structure of cheese.

ED COLETTI

The Notion of Wings

It's the notion of
wings, that's what it is
More like flight the concept
or flying, a verb
Have you ever flown a verb?
Poets and lovers fly verbs all the time.
It's the exhilaration, that's what it is
straddling the latest verb soaring
bareback rider rodeoing space
landing with a thud, hard realization
rodeoing now requires redoing.
Shake off the stardust, mount up anew.
It's the notion of wings and flying the verbs
That's what it is.

JENNIFER COMPTON

The Pursuit of Poetry

Once you have become a drug addict
you will never want to be anything else

- Dransfield

It's late afternoon. It's always late afternoon.
Take what you will want. Walk out the door.
Walk towards the setting sun. Of course it means
turning away from the people you are leaving
with cold eyes, unamenable cold eyes.
Never say goodbye.

Now you have walked out of the house where everything
means too much. Now you are walking up the street until
you don't know where you are. Abandon what you thought
you wanted to carry. You are becoming unclean forgetting
the passwords walking like dancing talking without meaning
back under the moon you never thought you'd see again speaking

in a voice you haven't heard in a long while
guessing *lamp post* guessing *moon* something
jerks twitches flutters something falls down —
there is the next front door right there.
It's very important to walk towards the setting sun.
And to never tell where you have been. What you have done.

JENNIFER COMPTON

Instructions for Open Mic Sessions

Don't moan like second stage labour
in the back row. It doesn't help

anyone. Soften your eyes, like a horse,
so you can see everything at once

like they do. Understand the source
from which all this verse springs.

Intuit it. As if you lived in a village.
One day they'll die. In the meantime

they have a voice.
Their courage

as their arms swing and eyes roll
is their poem.

And the moment when they stall and
understand that on the richter scale

they are registering less than ten
is more moving than Fern Hill.

ANNE CORAY

For the Small Poem

Now the hand brushes the page
whose lips are soft as a newborn baby's.
She has just begun to breathe, to discover
the throat, the tongue, and her first sounds
burble up, contralto. It is all
we can do, to watch the phonic rungs
form their companionway to this vast deck
stacked with syllables and echoes.
What shall she make of it?
Water, we say, and point, and she says *water*,
a little softer, a little slower,
as the dawn spreads in full light on her brow;
she is not ours, this child,
who totters into outstretched arms.

ANNE CORAY

Ars Poetica

Nothing can be said
that is intended.

You cannot grow melons
but you learn that swamp grass
is of equal value.

If you should exact
the sound of a dove
you are perhaps unfortunate.
The coo must become
something slightly
undefined and private.

Deference to the self
is the only way to patience.
Is the slug unhappy
because he has no followers?

If you believed once in water
(whether oceans or tears)
you will someday uncover salt.
You will learn how it is mined,
begin a study of structure.

Curiously, you'll find the tongue
reluctant to accept a formal logic.

What you tend, after all,
is invariably simple:
a leaf, a blade, a stone,
the vowels long and pure,
rich and lovely.

ALISON CROGGON

―――――

Ars Poetica

It will make no difference.
But you'll find you can't speak without love
although it's an imprisonment.
Your voice must be love wrestled to unloving,
the lyre at the moment of catastrophe, a silence
within which another voice opens.

You'll speak as you must, as always,
although you'll never know why you're listening
through the elisions of your stuttering heart.
You'll long to finish, although nothing has happened,
although you haven't begun, as if your mere being
hurt you with abundance. No one will explain.

There are wounds that blind you, sudden voices
splitting into winter, toothed windows, terrors
sifting through white slumbers of corruption,
the wraith that greets you with your shrinking face
at dawn, anonymous and violent,
waiting for Virgil.

Because you have tasted your salt in the blood
of another's mouth, because a small flower
is eating the history of stone,
because you are asleep and all possibility
tilts on the edge of your vision, because you are nameless
and are called, because you know nothing ―

a possible music
lifts through the panic of dismay ―
it's the blue of all the flowers of your body,
the brain stem, the clitoris, the tongue,
the wrist vein, the channels of the heart, the dying lips,
reaching to their likeness in the sky, in the sky's waters ―
you can't lift it out of your flesh
because it won't exist, but it flowers past you.
It opens the places you've always been,

house, fire, glass, bed, water,
tree, night,
the child's glance which strews your transparencies
across a field of colours you have no name for,
the profane ash of touch
darkening your tongue, the dream of imperishable silver
which wakes to another dream, a boat departing
from an unmapped shore, and your crumbling words, unable
to hold even one drop of light.

Poems

The hack of putting pen to paper
in order to park a record of existence
is a screwball comedy.
It's a nuisance and charms me.
A happy red blister on the thumb of my face.
I mean it's an instance,
like saying "I was here." Or more at
"I am here." No probably less at that.

The crack of writing is always an act.
"I write less words than I hues to."
Always the yellow road is less cold
with a bullet in my ink.
My poems are pretty good
when I have a nice transmission.
I drive through the crack like a distance,
scribbling little bruises into the median.
Tiny little ears of ink settle upon each tissue of flimflam
until there's a whole book of em.

I hack in order to park
on an instant. Sometimes even parallel,
which is great fun
and can often result in a haxident.

CRAIG CZURY

White Pall

for Regina writing her exit

but for the death of each word
it's this white pall of the page i must bear

white pillow of the page

that leads me to [poetry?]

luxurious open space

for my eyes to rest

~

quiet enough to listen

to see what's listened to beyond

nothing to do with thinking

~

a private language written in a secret handwriting

~

this strained white tension of silence

for my words to blurt

~

but how can i not help erase myself

in the ridiculousness of

ink the embalming fluid of

words the sarcophagi of

thought the death of

knowing

    ridicule

~

what if by greeting each other

we speak poetry

what if our language upon arrival

breaks down into profound syllables of seeing

i mean seeing each other as an ecstatic first moment

and when we part

as if we'll never see each other again

~

inhuman and obscene

breaking the dreaminess of your morning thoughts

reading a newspaper

~

as seldom as i see you

your death with me is ok

i know you are always where you're supposed to be

our conversation continues

the look you give me continually guides/chides

~

stretched out on the beach

i am the horizon

stretched out on my bed of sand

cry of gulls rolling slamming surf

as the horizon i will also be forever

CRAIG CZURY

Uncovering The Mine Shaft

by accident
we stumbled upon the last breath
and knelt down
our one good ear tight against its lips
and rotted teeth

we could not tell
if it was night or the eclipsing sun

but from somewhere deep within its wound
we heard drums
and a circle of clapping bones closing in

again the woolly mammoth being roused
from its black slumbering dust

crude figures of men with sticks
and mud-sling barrows
illumined the cankerous mouth

YOKO DANNO

behind the words

written at all hazard
despite riots, curfews and typhoons
is a language unheard-of,

the language of fish
painted on the arched ceiling
of an ancient shrine,
revived by a touch
of salt water,

spoken as well by trees and animals
in a blind younger world
before literate humans arrived,

when a leaf was heavier than gold
            and silver dust still falling
                        from the moon —

a story starts
at the center behind a seer's eyes —

child monks parrot the words
diligently
with tears in their eyes —

from the bottom
of a salt lake,
dry and long forgotten,

rises a faraway laughter
like a ripple of mirage over water —

LUCILLE LANG DAY

If the Poem Is Broken,
How Can the Sunflowers Breathe?

They can't. The desert sunflower,
the slender sunflower,
Nutall's sunflower,
the Kansas sunflower
and the California sunflower
will all hang their heads.
Stomata will close
on diamond-shaped,
lancelike, and oval leaves.
You must help me keep
the poem intact
to let the sunflowers breathe.

DENISE DUHAMEL

My First Book of Poetry
Was Like My First Baby

since I don't plan to have children. I wanted people to love it
and make a fuss, and, in turn, tell me what a great job I'd done.
My book wasn't reviewed in that many places, and when it was,
one reviewer even called it sloppy. The grandparents weren't as doting
as I'd expected. They went on with their own lives
and didn't buy the book any presents. No one took a picture of me
holding the book in my lap. My husband wasn't jealous
that I was spending too much time with the book. My dog
sniffed the book and walked away, unthreatened. Other books
were getting cooed and fussed over, books cuter and more enchanting than mine.
There is no greater pain for a mother — seeing her child left out. Soon I knew
I had a book that would never accomplish much with its life,
that it wouldn't win prizes or be displayed in prestigious bookstores.
That my book would probably be a drop-out, that I'd have nothing
to brag about when my cousins showed me graduation pictures of their kids.

That my book wouldn't buy me dinner or take care of me
when I grew old. I tried not to let the book sense my disappointment.
I tried to love it for the book that it was, but it began to have the telltale signs
of depression, hanging out with the wrong crowd,
dressing like a rebel. The book reminded me of myself as a teenager,
but when I told it that it shivered in disgust, blaming me
for bringing it into this world in the first place.

PATRICK JAMES DUNAGAN

I Haven't Even Told You Who I Am

I work in the back room, planting igloos.
I came to this occupation with no set purpose.
I heard they were hiring and applied, dreaming
    "adventures on ice."
I believe I wooed the boss with my tall tales and
    heroic looks.

Most mornings I drink coffee and rest easy.
Most begin without deliberate end.
Most remain inside as I go out.
Most would cite obscure texts and leave it at that.

As if I wasn't aware, alive in all this wet heat.
As if igloos.
As if in old photos the halls of my youth.
As if ever.

Here's the thing: this isn't going anywhere.
Here's the thing, quote,
"Here's the thing. Believe in what's said or don't. It
    won't change anything."
Here's the thing: I no longer believe in this particular
    thing.

RICCARDO DURANTI

———

The ambush

The light is waiting
    flexible and jagged
at the end of the passage.

This elastic ink
is getting there again
slowly, unaware.

It becomes crisp and alive
for a moment:
a clear-cut tree
a hillful of trees
olive trees against a tramontana sky.

Then the ambush snaps.

Rippled and sucked
by a greedy south
ink and wind
are swallowed, whole.

Through the very gate, over the threshold
thoughts and branches
words and leaves
bones and pebbles
flesh and soil
melt together in a silent sigh:
they acknowledge with a chill
the power
that deals them such a light death
and then delivers their ghosts
into a black & white flat heaven ...

Content

Not wrenched, but rendered —
extract beyond word or image:
matter melted into mind into matter melting,
tongue telling eye
seeing melt of mind beyond matter,
eye mattering as mouth does,
here much more than ear
ever than an h is,
ere eye sees y.

Why an ear sees here
more than eyes hear there
is what a paradox is.

A mouth mattering
as word or image.
An eye's as much an ear:
look, hear beyond mutter of fact.

PAUL DUTTON

Why I Don't Write Love Poems

In love, too busy.

And out, too caught
by poetry's essence:
yearning.

PAUL DUTTON

Missed Haiku

In the only room that matters
a slight sound
obscures the one thought that counts.

SUSANNE DYCKMAN

what to leave

an island paradise off course

a lemon or a willow branch battered by the wind

all tangible proof   certain as the fabric spun by worms

slowly

leave this behind

forgiveness for the dead

who are growing repetitious

the untenable freedom of birds

a testament of thieves

Workshop Poem; or, Sorry, Austin

One participant said saxophones
are always being asked to do
too much work in poems.

They are always there growling about
sex, and cigarettes smoking alone, it seems
to me. And so, she objected. Another woman

felt that way about cicadas. You know,
she said, they're always there in the background
with their dizzy wings, the infernal saw

of Georgia nights, or Mississippi, or some
godawful Southern swamp. They never work.
Sorry. For me, offered the last, it's bougainvilleas.

And they all agreed. The heavy-scented,
head-filling veil of their pungency, wafting
or whatever, across the veranda, it's predictable.

And then there's that thing about Vietnam,
the association with the Mekong Delta, or bombs,
or I don't know, but bougainvilleas are just

too much. And so there we were, with
the cicadas and the saxophones and the bougainvilleas
roaring around the table, the poem

flat and quiet between us. Our work
here is done, one announced. Thank you
for the generosity of your words.

Varnish This!

The worst color and two coats
of it thick on the desk
that I want for my work. Three
kinds of stripping solution, steel wool,
turpentine, finally de-natured
alcohol does the trick, lifts
malignant stain from the deep grain,
gives me back the lines
of raw wood, corners grey and rough
where damage must be scrubbed smooth.
But now it is my desk; I own
its very skin, have claimed its planed surface,
brace, and drawer with chafed hands,
stiff neck, cramped back stooped
to abrade its dark belly, squared legs.
And hard varnished to slick
and shining surface, I set my light,
my book, my clean sheets,
dangerous points upon it, and when asked
about my work I say: *If
you want to write, then do it.*

Ars Poetica

The man who thought the ocean a bull
rode out to red horizon.
The ocean threw off a corpse
stiff as water was not.

It lay flat in the stadium of noon
where a bull tossed over its horns
a death no less real than the ocean.

ANNIE FINCH

———

Interpenetrate

Like the bleached fibers and their haunted ink,
interpenetrate each others' solitudes,

not penetrating, not dissolving; stay
rolled with the single patterns of the days,

linking through pages to burn with speaking lace
and thread to bodies, evenly alive.

Nonce Sonnet 4

Make-
up's op-
portunities
to streak: rush
hour. The PA
system organizes
muck, and my luck
is behind one who'd
rather preempt humble
conjecture with a jeremiad
than reach his pristine bar or seedy
bower before the late show. The power
to tuck in high-tech earplugs is encouraged
by a paper friend unless I'm inclined to ride bass
lines below unmodulated treble. You might pluck
an expiring flower from the waiting room floor to save it
for an aspiring gatherer's open pouch. Where farming of image
is neither inherently devil (e.g. stealing from those presumed mute)
nor blessed delivery, where ouch is neither trounced nor deified, she'll
pitch a scrimmage for poetics. Where any ceiling is unafraid to fluctuate.

———

Ars Poetica
for Alec Finlay

The sayable
    in nouns
in syllables
    is nuance

As if a flock
    of small birds ate
the feeder but
    left the nuts

SHARON HARRIS

Experiment 99 a.

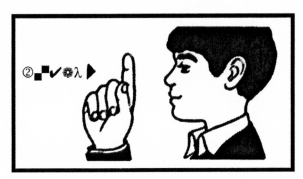

Experiment 99a. Where do poems come from?

Moisten your finger and hold it straight up in the air. You will notice at once that one side of the finger is cold. This is the direction from which the poem is coming.

LOLA HASKINS

His Poems

Some lie, pins set, pins set, in a field of plox, a living room,
the road to that store. The smallest contact and they explode;
hence the poet's country is full of the limbless.

Others, read without protection, whiten the watcher's eyes
instantly, so he spends the rest of his life in snow.

The poet's readers understand the risk, yet each book
he flings into the crowd lands in a pair of eager hands.

How can this be? Is this a trick the poet plays?
Who are these readers?
What can we do to bring them here?

LOLA HASKINS

Epitaph for a Poet

Here lies Richard.
He tried to improve on silence.

LOLA HASKINS

Sleep Positions

This is how we sleep:
On our backs, with pillows covering our chests, heavy as dirt
On our sides, like wistful spoons
Clenched, knees in-tucked, arms folded
Wide, like sprawling-rooted lotuses

In Iowa on top of pictures of Hawaii, huge white flowers on blue
In New York on black satin
In China on straw.

This is how our dreams arrive:
As hot yellow taxicabs
As sudden blazing steam, we who have been pots on a stove,
looking only at our own lids
As uninvited insects, all at once on our tongues.

Oh hairdresser, auditor, hard-knuckled puller of crab traps,
you who think poetry was school, you who believe
you never had a flying thought,
lie down.

NELLIE HILL

All Day, Pen Poised

This is how you get the poem.
You sit in the boat just offshore.
You cast — a whine as the sinker plunges.
Water slaps the boat's sides gently.
Voices drift from a cottage,
plunkety plunk on a summer piano,
toward evening a loon's cry,
and the silent beaver swimming their way
to some secret place.
Which is the poem — the thick-mouthed bass
you fling into the boat or the sounds
that foretold his arrival?

NATHAN HOKS

Spatula Mouth

When one holds a spatula
to the lighted light bulb, the silhouette
zooms away. The silhouette burns
a mouth inside the mouth. The mouth
burns an engine in the silhouette.
With this mouth you might say:
silhouette yourself. With this mouth
you might make other mouths.
You might spend four days kissing.
You might sing and eat at the same time.
This mouth does not fear
the street-sweepers, the meter-maids,
the parking attendants who weave
quilts out of left-behind seatbelts.
With this mouth a bird rises and flares out,
the wind swims by like seaweeds,
an electrical charge and the wind
and a lantern around your neck.
Mouth around your neck. Spatula
piercing the delicate skin of your pocket.
E-mails my thumb, inserts pills in small plastic case.
The silhouette comes back like a cape.
Mouth eats poem. Falls from rafters.
Light bulb beside house, house up in flames.

PAUL HOOVER

Rehearsal in Black

The science of the irrational,
poetry knows what time is feeling
in the language we speak. Casual

as a crow above the pealing
tower, it circles our point of view
with applied indifference. The ceiling

is the limit only in the room;
love is torn between two sheets;
animals eat each other. Truth

is another order, beyond the heat
of sense. The memory of language
is a blind cold wall, a sweet

old man carrying a doll, pages
of silence framed by the chase.
What is love's name in an age

of skin? Everything you face
is just as it happened, minus all
the details. You write a line a day,

whether bad or good, then fall
into a stupor. A line of black cars
arrives at the horizon. In the fall,

you've noticed, the fattest stars
get even fatter. Maybe it's the air,
sodden with nostalgia. We are

what we are, a kind of rare
poison steeped in a kiss. Roots,
reeds, fish, the broken river —

everything is perfectly suited
for a local drowning. Here's a shot
of the water surface, with its mute

tensions and the struggle not
to fold. The world, dispersing,
turns. Here's the face of a god

no one remembers, in the church
of words. The American laugh,
said Jung, is urgent as a thirst.

It bowls you over with its raffish
humor and grabs you by the balls.
You can see the diver's glove, half-

filled with blood, in the halls
of that museum, where nothing
finally matters but stands as tall

as it can. Life is always touching
the edges of a net. Light enters water,
and that is called perspective. Such ends

are met when language and space, neither
quite sufficient, negotiate a realm.
It's cold inside, children have no fathers,

and mothers are desperate to tell
of love. It's a landfill country, strewn
with cast-off things, where stone bells

ring and drowned boats rise. The truth
is confused but strikes for the prize:
the stone floor of the sea, red tooth

of existence, and what the eyes deny.
You descend the stairs to hell, walk
its plazas and parks, and manage to find

a date for the evening. She talks
of her desires, but this is not desire;
it's the tender mercy of a leaf's awkward

falling. At what firm margin, the fires
in the mirror or in your eyes, is love
to be found? Does the sea aspire

to be just water? In the weave of
your intentions, the air plays the air.
Nothing is nothing. In a coven

of mechanics, in the scariest
Hollywood mansion, love is the prize
and a touch of the fever. Rare

as existence, it has seen the mind
change the most desolate landscapes
into quiet rooms. It always finds

the world in absence, doors taped
shut. This is like the movies, a black
room filled with murmurs. As the drapes

are pulled, you see from the back
life's enormous figures falling in
and out of focus, a final slackness

of being we later enjoy enduring.
The story is stained with its own
rehearsal. A handsome bed is burning.

Serious and alluring, a long dial tone
passes for conversation. No one's
there but you, talking into the phone

like a younger father to an older son.

PAUL HOOVER

Edge and Fold XLI

XLI

> *where is a written deer*
> *running through a written forest*
>
> — *Wisława Symborska*

the written man in bed
      with his unwritten wife

she who has written
      his figure in that place

experience that lives
      only in the written

a dark brown mouse
      crossing to the mirror

vacant fishermen
      staring into ponds

as if to write them
      naked with indifference

what is fire writing
      in the house of darkness

all inner space imagined
      nothing in shadow

everything that is
      written by what is not

—

Poetry is

the antidote to the poison of rationality; the best friend
entropy ever had; the botany of the impossible wedded
to the chemistry of the ineffable; the jewel in the heart
of the flotsam; the mote in the eye of the lotus; the
canary in the mind. Or else, to lift an image from one
old poet, it is "all the history of grief" consolidated into
"an empty doorway and a maple leaf." Or perhaps it is
a vision of the mugs on Mount Rushmore, aeons
hence, eroding into long, mournful portraits by the
geological equivalent of Modigliani; or that of two
crows perched on a withered limb, just across the
street from the county seat. Or maybe it is simply
the antique urgency of this mouth moving at this
moment, with all these other mouths, continuing to
shape and tune a common tongue, a common song,
leaping from the body into someone's arms, or head,
or breakfast, leaping into the very air that mothered
it in the lungs, dancing and leaping even as we sleep,
even as we sag, bend, curdle, and vote Republican

RAY HSU

Note on Cooking

*Someone has observed that a pig resembles a saint
in that he is more honored after death than during
his lifetime. Speaking further of his social standing,
we have noticed that, when smoked, he is allowed to
appear at quite fashionable functions; but that only
one's best friends will confess to anything more
than a bowing acquaintance with pork and
sauerkraut or pickled pigs' feet.*
— The Joy of Cooking

One morning language thought me. I collected its thoughts over
breakfast and sorted them into loose characters. Were they friends?
I copied their words. *God helps those who help themselves,* one
said. Did I hear that right? Did I cross it out carefully? *Is self-help
the opposite of self-reliance?*

Jacques Lacan liked to think of psychosis as when you don't
quite understand the language you're speaking. Did I mean other
people? I said language. Others thought about me in different
ways than I thought about myself. They pointed out what was
written on my face. I tried to be coherent, but met versions of me
that had been invented by others. *Because he doesn't know who
he is,* the Tao Te Ching tells us, *people recognize themselves in
him.* They were my teachers. They taught me what I could be. We
are real and imaginary.

They followed me on the Greyhound bus to Wisconsin. Michael
Taussig tells us that the power of the copy is the power to
influence what it is a copy of. I studied others' inventions of me
and extracted ingredients from them. Then something about me
changed.

To experiment, I need to judge what has worked and what hasn't.
Taste is a good way to judge. If I don't have taste, then I need
people with taste, to taste. Is it selectivity that makes good art?
Tastes tell us about desire. I like reading my tastes: they show
me how I consume. They also show how others consume me. *A
swordsman should not have a favorite sword,* Miyamoto Mushashi
thought. I like to think that I have no taste.

Over time, my characters developed many interesting facts. In a room, I copy down two that are scattered throughout this book. [1][2]

To both of these, I hear my mother think of me. *Food is the one thing that you must ensure is good because it gets in your body*, she'd say.

[1] *The last time I taught creative writing, each student had written an average of ninety-two pages over fifteen weeks, which was more than I had asked for.*

[2] *One of my students in prison wrote an essay that was good enough to be in the 95 percentile of all my campus students. His teacher and principal tried to use his writing to reform a section of the prison. But some view change as a threat: someone put copy of essay in his file, probably the head of security, and this essay will mark him as a trouble-maker from now on. Do I want to change things for the better, even if it risks my students? I couldn't sleep because I couldn't remember whether that I had left his writing behind where a guard or administrator might find it.*

HALVARD JOHNSON

Maglev Sonnet

A high-speed magnetic sonnet went off its track
in northwestern Germany on Friday, killing at least
one passenger and injuring several more, sources said.

Officials at the scene described the sonnet's first stanza
as being totally mangled. "We must prepare ourselves
for the fact that those lines are not living any more,"

said one critic, who shall forever remain nameless.
He was talking to emergency officials. Besides those
first-stanza lines, two other quatrains were missing

and feared dead. How fast the sonnet was traveling
at the time of the accident was not immediately clear.
Eighteen tropes are still trapped in tangled wreckage.

The accident is another blow for magnetic levitation
after a fire last month in a Shanghai-bound ghazal.

JILL JONES

Things to make and do

Waver on stilts while listening to arias.

Sew your own rose and ask of its questions.

Steal flotsam like wanton flies.

Ruin lyrics, while above the egrets lift.

Paste green language around a cork room.

Refuse to 'nail it'. Just refuse.

Keep rearranging what is footnote and what is space.

Walk out one day in presences.

Release the necessary angels from their curators.

Make friends with adverbs, unwisely.

Take night's immediate nerve with possibility.

Speculate outside with the big southerly.

Pass as you go into.

Sleep all around at blue windows.

Burn down the villa, change all the doors.

Stand so shadows make you perfect.

Love your dumb corpus, of song.

ADRIANNE KALFOPOULOU

Growing

She uses the apartment keys
to let herself in from the neighbor's.
I am unnerved, maybe from drinking.
I know it will take all
the last of my strength to get through
the bath hour, reading *Babar*,
the talk of hair, how and if we will braid it,
tomorrow's homework review —
I am really in a poem I say, cutting
lines together, images, this poem
I am always aiming at, pulling the sheet over
the day's trial, pulling browned buds
from the night flower (didn't give it enough
water this winter — it might not bloom
this spring). Brushing out
my daughter's fine hair over her
wide forehead, caressing it, I put
another story together; she says
in eight-year-old-directness, "You threw him out
didn't you?" This is the moment
I gather the lines, the poem, the raw
tendrils, watered or not, snapped in urgency
(the night flower has such a pungent smell).
"He wasn't with me anymore sweetie,
he slept on the couch in the living room,
that's not being together." She weighs this,
the poem, in fragments, may never get written.
We are managing this — I am calm, I am on
other territory, a kitchen of plenty,
school problems solved, pencils sharpened,
the lesson memorized. "Did I do it right?"
she asks of the math review, I am calculating the lesson —
Motherhood, this sudden test. Unprepared,
untutored I am telling her the grade isn't important,
it's what you learn, what you can take with you.

BHANU KAPIL

Notes from the Padded Chair

(I've been thinking lately about the esophageal tract — the relationship of sound to poetry. And how a hand on the throat, in desire as in violence, is real. But if poetry is written in a third space, some place less obvious than the colors blue or red, then where is that space? I contend that it is metallic, off-white and filled with women. There are soft lights and a faint odor of chilled peppermint liqueur. So what about Loveland Family and Cosmetic Dentistry on North Cleveland Avenue? As a venue. Venue 1, for these parallel notes.)

I am writing this on a dentistry pad. The kind in a wicker basket on the receptionist's banquette. Is that a word? I want a blanket, there on the reclining chair. And hold it open with your fingers. And wire it open like a jaw. Now I'm shivering. Are you shivering? Can I get you a quilted coverlet or a bolster for your neck? Please keep your hands where I can see them at all times. Just relax. But I like it. I like to receive an altering touch. To the mouth, to the teeth, the soft as to the hard. Yep, I'd like to book my next appointment.

Venue 2: A room, the next street over. I'd like to keep going, but that would be to fantasize. Something about poetry keeps you in the padded chair, where you belong: irradiated, legless, smiling witlessly and yet with ardor at the strangers who surround you when you wake up from a deep, deep sleep. They're asking you something but something about about poetry makes you drool and respond, in fragments of your true speech. I don't know if it's poetry. Are you normal? Are you a conventional patient who's come prepared with a supply of kleenex tucked into the sleeve of your cardigan? No. Clearly, you're not. You should go home. I'm going to call you a cab, ma'am. You're in no condition to drive.

W. B. KECKLER

What is Poetry?

"... that which cannot be paraphrased?"
Well, so is a rock. Scissors. Paper.
Rock. Scissors. Paper. Mind.

Put your hands behind your back.
Just cup your palm for mind.
Choose one of the four. Be sly.

One. Two. Three. *Go.*
Paper beats rock. Wraps it up,
as history's lines wrap lies. We're stoned.

One. Two. Three. *Show.*
Scissors cuts mind into paper dolls.
(Descartes throws up before multiplied I's.)

One. Two. Three. *Whoa.*
Mind beats rock, beats against rock
until world relents, and the matter settles

grit on the tongue. Two. Three. *So.*
Paper slices mind in tissue samples,
soul's salami, soul's Salamis of utter

defeat to a Kleenex-thinness of thinking,
*how can a tornado drive a piece of straw
through a roof beam?* But deep down

you know, you really know how,
if you've ever played the game before.
If you ever saw a page behead someone,

yet leave the heart furiously beating.
This is the praying mantis, death-in-life,
which leaps from leaf to leaf, life to life

and the dead all turn their heads
360 degrees when they are inside it.
And lovers are the only ones will ride it.

KARL KEMPTON

Of Ink
for Karl Young

1. A

As the first letter
was made like a pyramid
tomb of alphabet birth

2. 4 i's

Inkwell sun behind horizon
the scribe of dusk
dips the quill
to dot night's i

Venus

≈≈≈≈

The desire
to dot the i of air

from which
they

as birds
would become

dinosaurs invent
the feather

≈≈≈≈

The i has been cast
head floats above body

What we have become
the vanishing points
the planet falls through

~~~~

By holding the e handle of ode
Crow dips the o
in the soapy water of Gnosis
and blows the bubble he flies into
as the dot that completes Nothing

3. The Third Eye

Himalayan yogi saints
to complete the perfect
continental cursive i's
float from mountain top to mountain
top
diacritic diadem bindu beacons

4. The others

Of the slingshots
u more difficult
to hold than y
pulling diacritic ammo

5. A calligraphy

Night's calligrapher
sharpens his quills
in the solar wind
the meteor lines

~~~~

Standing on Venus
feather with crescent moon hat

Writing with sunlight

~~~~

Laying lines on ocean at night
the planets sing of sun light

Comes a Time in a Poet's Life

when she writes
the prerequisite
blackberry poem
taking on the indelible
words of the famous.
I'll have none of it
substitute pussy
for pail and savor
ripest berry
coming soft/wet
in my mouth.

TRACY KORETSKY

———

Ars Poetica

Fiction is a bungalow —
preferably camouflaged,
with a high wit wind whistling through.
There is something in the attic
and someone about to ring the bell.

But a poem
        a poem,
                it is a cathedral.
Still air
        rising,
                ringing
                the vaults;
finials,
        pinnacles,
                pointing,
and all the little angels
        looking down.

        Between boughs, between even
        the teeth of pine cones, or seaming
        the backs of new blades, poems
        are in the name Forget-Me-Not, in the Sioux
        meaning "singing river" or the French
        for "silent mountain." They are the knowledge
        of a bird, its name, and journey,

While Fiction verbs from noun to noun
conflict crashing into crisis
determined to make good time, Poetry's
got its thumb out, its eyes upon the sky.

The Basement

A friend tells me on the phone she drank a glass of wine
one night and wrote, years and years ago, and the stuff

that bubbled out from her subconscious scared her so
she swore she'd never do that again. She was going to tell me

some story about Berryman but we had to get off the phone so I
never heard it, nor did I get a chance to tell her I wrote

half the stuff I've done drunk — at least by her yardstick.
But what *should* bubble up is the stuff from the subconscious

so I never really figured that out — why else would
you write poems if you weren't trying to get downstairs

into the basement, where the sewage pipes are all
covered with dust and mouse shit more ancient than death

and the corners you poke around in are just as likely to reveal that
soft spot you always had for, say, pornography, to be the dead

body of your brother rotting with the lost ten-penny nails
and some rusty washers, rolls of solder strips underneath

the workbench? Or that rat that ran across the shadows —
isn't that your father's anger at everything that went wrong

in his life transformed into your own? That hammers your
fists on the desk at the littlest frustration and howls like a
             rabid dog

at your daughter who's just bugging you for fun *Can't you see
that I'm angry?* as though that was some sort of accomplishment

to be proud of like the mitered box you made for your 4-H
butterfly project? Isn't that bull snake that made one mistake to
             look

for cool in the basement but found its own private hell, that mother's
hacked into bits with a garden hoe — the only time you remember her

coming down into the basement — enough to know she was killing
something that you didn't even know yet what it might be?
        The bathroom

where father sneaked off to smoke cigarettes, and your brother poked
        holes
in the shower to spy on your sister? The cubbyhole where he stashed

his *Playboys* and half pints of gin you discovered as if by a miracle?
Isn't this where your life began? Isn't this where you found yourself?

The Poem as Airplane Passenger

At first it's really nothing,
idling in the terminal, too poor
for overpriced bar drinks,
marked-up fast food.

It has explored in every direction,
the numbing repetition of gates,
their waiting crowds growing
from the lines of linked seats.

Soon it will board. But now,
poem slumps in a vinyl seat,
a foot propped up
on the carryon bag.

First called to board, it takes
an aisle seat. Other passengers
bump its waiting head
with bags as they go by.

A large man squeezes in
the window seat next to it,
spills over the armrest, gains
weight on the tarmac,

his shoulder forces poem's
torso into the aisle.
The flight attendant's ass
brushes poem's shoulder

as she checks the security
of every passenger's seat belt,
readies the cabin for takeoff.
Poem is uncomfortable,

but says nothing. Takeoff
awaits. The plane will rise,
air pressures change,
turbulence jar this narrow world.

In this new atmosphere,
Poem will grow, its body
become something new,
filling every empty space.

AMY LEMMON

———

Revival

Some lines seem destined for the nearest landfill
— the way my name, when I type the wrong keys,
becomes "Ant." I feel like an ant these days,
lugging my giant crumb to some great sand-hill,
dumping it, and trudging off for more.
I wonder where my good old-fashioned brain went?
It didn't fit my head, like the attachment
I bought second-hand for my vacuum cleaner.

You can't do much good with a bad connection —
part A fits into part B, no exceptions,
or you're screwed. There's no great adapter
to plug into, turn on the juice, the power
and the glory. Forever and ever, we survive,
trying dead sockets till something sparks alive.

Disclaimer

If you are reading this

it is due to an error,

an oversight, or some otherwise

unprecedented act on the part

of the Management.

blame it on the Moon

Do not be alarmed if

you hear a voice you are not accustomed to,

screams

or if mention is made of subjects

embarrassing nipples

out of your ordinary purview,

"those stubborn bloodstains"

or if unfamiliar territory is mapped

intricately and with candor.

that Moon, she brings —

Comfort yourself with the fact that

if not blood, then at least —

you will soon be returned

to your regularly scheduled programming,

"sorry, sorry, sorry"

with the requisite words from Our Sponsor.

Unless, of course, you prefer

To follow me away to the roof

hair curled to frame the face

to watch the white disk turn two-thirds

Lillian Gish on film, 1915

mottled sepia, then charcoal, then black,

then shyly bare her sharp white face entire.

LYN LIFSHIN

———

To Poem or,

Today You're Like a Phone I Almost

Don't Answer

21 feet high in
Philadelphia, the
no poem deep
quiet, the
February snow
peeling away. I'm
sitting near glass
pulled into sun, into
this poem

    somehow far

off un-
real like those
roofs down there, the
small cars. Poem,
you're like a
phone I almost
don't answer

putting its mouth
on me, a
voice I'd been
looking for and then
half avoided

Meet me in an hour

It's always yes

DIANE LOCKWARD

My Husband Discovers Poetry

Because my husband would not read my poems,
I wrote one about how I did not love him.
In lines of strict iambic pentameter,
I detailed his coldness, his lack of humor.
It felt good to do this.

Stanza by stanza, I grew bolder and bolder.
Towards the end, struck by inspiration,
I wrote about my old boyfriend,
a boy I had not loved enough to marry
but who could make me laugh and laugh.
I wrote about a night years after we parted
when my husband's coldness drove me from the house
and back to my old boyfriend.
I even included the name of a seedy motel
well-known for hosting quickies.
I have a talent for verisimilitude.

In sensuous images, I described
how my boyfriend and I stripped off our clothes,
got into bed, and kissed and kissed,
then spent half the night telling jokes,
many of them about my husband.
I left the ending deliberately ambiguous,
then hid the poem away
in an old trunk in the basement.

You know how this story ends,
how my husband one day loses something,
goes into the basement,
and rummages through the old trunk,
how he uncovers the hidden poem
and sits down to read it.

But do you hear the strange sounds
that floated up the stairs that day,
the sounds of an animal, its paw caught
in one of those traps with teeth of steel?
Do you see the wounded creature
at the bottom of the stairs,
his shoulders hunched over and shaking,
fist in his mouth and choking back sobs?
It was my husband paying tribute to my art.

RUPERT MALLIN

Made Up Poem

With brush, pencil and stick her poem makes an appearance:
A made up, out of bed, out of the shower, out there poem;
An eye-lined, lip lush, highlighted bright poem;
A 'go to work on a poem' kind of poem;
A lady luck club loving poem;
A made up poem.

With cream, tissue and water her poem makes an
appearance:
An indoors, into the shower, into her bed poem;
A red-eyed, lip cracked, pasty poem;
A 'real me' poem;
A broken poem.

Tossing, turning, sweating, her poem makes an appearance:
The boat of her life is ever sinking
And family and friends always knew she had pulled the plug
And her favourite brush is matted with hair
And try as she does she can't pull this terrible poem
From its teeth, from her appearance, but ...

With brush, pencil and stick her poem makes an appearance:
A made up, out of bed, out of the shower, out there poem;
An eye-lined, lip lush, highlighted bright poem;
A 'go to work on a poem' kind of poem;
A lady luck club loving poem;
A made up poem.

PAMELA McCLURE

Ars Poetica

Shucked mussels in cellophane, workers tossing
Squares of sod onto the suburban yard
In front of the new, pastel house
Where there have been only two lights on at dusk.

Snow on the gun's nose, snow on the shoulders
Of the Latin scholar leaving the library dust
Behind her, shaking loose her hair

As if the line drawn by the worker to place
The banister more than line, but
An arrow fixed and pointing to the dipper's cup

And the eternal song: all done for the listening ear
Of the hunchback turning toward the magnolia
Blossom unfurled in the window. He turns his sad

Face to the outside, and strolls away, leaning
Into the avenue of opposites, music
From the open throats of mutes, or wind seen
In the maculate mouths of the fluted

Lily. All poison, all trembling to unearth us.

D. H. MELHEM

On the tendency toward solipsism
in literature

1.
Where am I in your poems?
How can you be there without
the boundary defining you — the place
we are accomplishing? Are you
a blob, unmanageable endless omnivore,
a science fiction fact, the total topographical
of earth, a mobile constellation, quirky quasar,
voluminous vegetal omniscient —
how about that?
Where are you leading — except
to Parmenides, his circle
spherically flat?

2.
The unimpassioned poem is retrospective of a flight
responsible only to
its own hovering images that link
Ming vases with the tense
of made things, of mental surfaces, and with feelings
shaped to the fixed glaze of a tight, washable glisten.
Feathers can dust the unimpassioned poem
where nothing
importunately clings

but the poem whose rude textures
grapple with the live space
around the self
can grip the air
and hold light, and fly
as the earth flies

HILARY MELLON

White Ink

(for George Szirtes - il miglior fabbro)

Your white ink settles on my page like snow
My stuttered words are quivering in the creases
Snow settles on my words and smothers them
My white ink clings to margins and to edges
Your white ink glides across this shiny page
My words are stumbling through your drifts of snow
Your snow has frozen all my white ink words
My white ink melts beneath your quiet breath
Your white ink lingers round my wordless mouth

PAUL MITCHELL

Woman Leaves Poetry Seminar

(for Kevin Brophy)

finished with the poetry thing
now I have to deal with
dirty nappies, screaming,
a husband who thinks poetry's quaint
but

where is it all leading?

there it goes
through the traffic
leaving a trail of tail lights
smudging up the rain

there it is
carved up on a butcher's tray
but not yet dead

& there it was
in the split of curtain
drawn down in Jesus' last words

the poetry thing is over
the reading, the talking
now for the living
where the bloody poetry thing
keeps on appearing

leading to places
where words are used
to describe what words cannot

& I'm a fool that tries

PAUL MITCHELL

Masterclass

It's no use showing me poems about music;
I'm tone deaf.

There's nothing wrong with that one,
just needs more brilliance.

Yeah, you've written a shocker there.

Having died you never completely come back.
I had a rehearsal for the big stage.

Great poem. And full of love.

*   Don't use tired images when you feel
        you are at a crucial point.

Don't crowd the idea. Have confidence
the point is made and

ask yourself
has this poem got hungry pockets?

CARLEY MOORE

Word Planet!

There's the waking up and being thrown out in the midst of words.
And then the words in the garden: the getting out, the go.
A rule of words, a pile of words.
Words stacked up (racked up) carelessly on a hill.
And words left behind but hanging off of trees.
Some words on the tip of a sword.
Some words still grim on t-shirts.
Words holding onto embankments while waiting and remembering.
Words in and out of place.
The unusual and glowering words-the tied up words.
The get-out-of-my-neighborhood-words.

But it's sudden.
It's the announcement, the way of seeing, newer words now
wrapped in spindled and gilded gold.
Word planet!
He wrapped the plants and columns in words
only to find those plants and columns unwrapped because of
words.
His wings encased in words that now work with precision.
No more wasted or useless words.
Words bound up in the telling fingers of an angel.
Words in blue and gold blankets and in ladies' chambers.
Words on walls with all the same thing to say.
The golden words coiled around the neck of the woman
and around the neck of the room.
The golden words are tight and tighter still at the tips of a thousand
feathers.

He will never be wordless.
The blue dress is a dome of words.
There are words hidden in slippers and bedclothes.
Words behind curtains and low stools.
Words written on the inside of eyelids and later sewn into books.

DANIEL THOMAS MORAN

At Hard Labor

I suppose I am grateful
that writing a poem

is not like mining sulfur
from the banks of a volcano

or welding a crossbeam
miles above the street.

Nor is it like
erecting a dreamhouse.

Most days, it is more
like splicing a phone line,

or hanging a door
on a linen closet.

Afterall, we live
in a world of toiling,

sweeping the dust
from the steps,

only to find them
wanting once more.

Wiping the gray mud
from our boots, then

walking out into the
field again at morning.

I have never
invited these poems, yet

they keep on arriving
one by one, shaking

the rain
from their shoulders

as they emerge from
the dark beyond my door.

I suppose I am grateful
that they did not

rob my house
or steal my children

from their
very beds.

Writing a poem
is not like

rising at first light
to cook for an army,

but more like
waking at ten on Sunday

to prepare an omelet
for someone you really love,

or teaching a small child
to lace up a shoe.

It is the dancers I pity,
who must aspire

to leap and spin, and
the painters who must

live with the burn of
turpentine in their veins.

What of the man
near the park, who stands

on the best days and the worst
turning chestnuts over tiny coals.

Or the waitress
who must always

be concerned with
what I want to drink.

Writing a poem is not
like any of that, I think.

But enough, the rain
is ferocious tonight,

So much that I fear
the hills will be washed away,

And if I am not mistaken,
there may be someone

at
my door.

Poetry

Poetry is the mysterious associate
    I introduce to a few
    friends and acquaintances.

Poetry wears an ascot to hide
    the throat hole, the source of the song
    since the operation.

Poetry is the enigmatic emissary,
    always difficult,
    always elusive.

Poetry is my comforter,
    wrapping a motley mantle
    about my swiveling ears.

Poetry is my lover —
    mine   only —
    though nothing is ever declared.

Poetry is my silent advisor,
pointing with trembling excitement
    to the flowering moon,
    to the green streaks in old granite.

Poetry is my inscrutable opponent
    putting tigers in my path,
    disturbing my earthly devotions.

Poetry is a courier of insight
    the journey often oblique,
    the message artful in its simplicity.

Poetry delivers its truth
    just as the oracle does,
    long after I have passed by.

RICHARD NEWMAN

Bar Poem

This poet walks into a bar, sits down,
and scribbles notes on a cocktail napkin.
The barkeep says, "Hey, did you know we named
a drink after you?" "Really?" the poet asks,
suddenly looking up. "No, but we figured
you'd be self-absorbed enough to believe it."
What cheap cocktails might a poet inspire?
Fuzzy Navel Gazer? Arse Poetica?

Last night a bunch of poets got together
here and read their poems against the war,
not realizing that most Americans
would see a night like "Poets Against the War"
as a good argument for taking up arms —
if not against Iraq against the poets.
Before he died, one of my best friends
asked me, "How many poets does it take
to screw in a light bulb? Two. One to write
about the light, the other to gaze out
the window." He was a photographer and knew
about the light, and teased me that the only
light I ever wrote about was Bud Light.
After my friend died, his wife asked me
to write a poem for his memorial,
which I read in front of a couple hundred mourners.
I felt like a creep capitalizing
on a captive audience, on my friend's death,
catapulting my poetic career,
such as it is or ever could be. Poet!

At the bar there's a flyer from the "Poets Against
the War" reading. On the back someone
has written, "Oh shut up" — no doubt another
poet impatient to take the podium.
The lights dim and the bar grows crowded. Shadows
crawl up the walls, and the bar grays with smoke.
I tip an Arse Poetica to my friend,
to those about to die in the coming war,
which poets won't stop since poetry best
helps the living when honoring the dead.

ANGELA ALAIMO O'DONNELL

Texas Tale

I went to Texas
and a town burnt down.

Believe it or not,
its name was Flat.

A poem waiting
to happen, I'd say.

Town with a name like
Flat just catching fire,

its scorched pines and pic-
nic benches crackling

in the noonday heat,
snapping into flame

like matchsticks on the soles
of some body's big boots.

It was a tall town,
Flat, before it burnt —

well — flat, and became
what it was meant to be.

Tall as a live oak
against the prairie.

Tall as a daughter
just before she leaves.

Tall as the Gulf Oil
sign at Wick Harney's

full-service station
at Main St. & First

in a small Texas
town that was once tall

till fire proved it proud
and cursed it flat.

One more Texas fact:
it never happened.

The town that burnt down
had another name,

one forgettable
and tragically true.

And I had nothing
to do with the fire.

But the poem came
anyway, a spark

some vague-eyed native
or half-deaf traveler

to Texas let drop
and laid to waste

a town that never
was and still is not

Flat as ever in the
level heart of Texas.

ANGELA ALAIMO O'DONNELL

Heresy

I'm an Italian woman and my poems say *Mangia!*
I want to feed you bread & wine, fruit & feast,
blessed and broken words to chew, chew, chew.

I want you to eat them purely for pleasure,
to put your lips around *p*,
crack *k*'s with your crowns,

roll *l*'s across your taste-budded tongue
to swallow sweet & easy
the meal of your life.

For it is what your body craves,
your heart sorely wants,
what your gut loves.

It is lies & truth, death & life,
sweet/sour, adazzle/dim,
what you have always and never known.

It is itself and you besides,
every thing & no thing at all.
It stuffs you full

and leaves you
heavy, hungry,
starved for more.

It makes you glad.
It troubles your sleep.
It is my body & my blood.

Here.
Take.
Eat.

SHIN YU PAI

Poem

for Wolfgang Laib

·a life
of collecting pollen
from hazelnut bushes
a life of gathering word-grains
to find all you have wanted
all you have waited to say

five
mountains
we cannot climb
hills we cannot touch
perhaps we are only here
to say house, bridge, or gate

a passage
to somewhere else
yellow molecules
spooned and sifted
from a jar filled with

sunlight
       pouring
              milk
       over
              stone
you are the energy
that breaks form
building wax houses
pressed from combs

a wax room
set upon a mountain
an offering of rice
nowhere everywhere
the songs of Shams

SHIN YU PAI

A conversation between
Huidobro and Braque

Is a poem a poem?
And isn't an orange just an orange,
and not an apple?

Yet next to each other, the orange
ceases to be orange
the apple ceases to be apple,
and together the two
become fruit.

HELEN PAVLIN

Metamorphosis of the Poet

Kangaroos, they say,
have the most efficient
water-conservation system.
You see them sip the dew
and know they'll not waste good water
flushing out their kidneys.

From novel to short story
to poem
I now require to distil
in ever more concentrated form.

In this age of conservation,
will there be those who want
the sparse
pellets of uric acid
I now produce?
Or do they only wish
to study the precise calibre of hair,
the porosity of bone
the fox-scats
which yield
biography,
appetite and habitat?

Frugal of future life, too
the kangaroo always carries
a foetus
ready to grow or not
as conditions permit.
Like a poem.

JOHNATHAN PENTON

Deep Throat Nihilism

Never forget that beauty is destructive

and poetry is its most destructive form

Poets do not ask permission

When you sing *Ave Maria* in the library, sing it loud

ALICE PERO

Found Poem

This is a poem on the back of the credit card slip
It can't help itself
It had to come into being
even though the meal is over and the dishes
cleared away
The poem is overwriting the check, crowding out the numbers,
elbowing its way past the clicking of the machines that
make perfect copies on computers
It has a lot to say; it scrambles over the TV screen and
spills onto another slip, the one from the post office
We are not commenting
The poem must have its way,
past the waitress pushing up the aisle with glasses of wine
past the crowds cheering the basketball players
The bread and butter lie in their beds, untouched
the poem hovers and falls, like a small leaf
in an errant wind
Who is listening?
The bird on the fence?
The man at the bar who had one too many?
Flip a coin.
Will the poem land again on a piece of pink paper?
Will it bounce, like the basketball
and fall in a dark corner
hidden by dust?
or will it rise again
speaking in tongues
above the earth where we find ourselves
breathing with the clouds
thin as the air

PATRICK PHILLIPS

———

Ars Poetica: Hitting the Curve

The only trouble with hitting a curve ball
is that your knees are in love with your skull.

To make them lean *towards* something someone
has flung with clenched teeth at your chin

you have to fake that your front-cleat is soaking
in an old milking pail. And believe for an instant

the truth isn't true — that even the Gods, even
Williams and Cobb, fail more often than not.

It helps to know Plato's *is* from *becomes* —
that the field was a *field*, the bat a creaking ash limb.

To know even your withered, pale father was beautiful
once, the bat falling from his shoulders like silk

as you lift your foot from the bucket and wail
like Achilles, without spilling a drop of the milk.

PAUL PINES

From: *Divine Madness*

The idea is to throw out a net of words
to catch the poem

a net such as Vulcan makes
at the ocean's depths
in a fiery cave
                    a net of fire in water
                    forged by one
                    cast out
                              cuckold of Venus
                              lame joke of the gods

 whose hairy blacksmith hands
can make a net such as Neptune wields
to hold the waves

                    a net of words
                    arching back on itself
                    to contain the exploded universe

a net of light cast into a galactic sea
of dancing stars

              a choreography of answers
              in a dark chamber
              where the soul
              is revealed

as a net of questions
in a net of breath

KEVIN PRUFER

There is No Audience for Poetry

They wanted him to stop kicking like that —
it made their eyes corkscrew, drilled the sun in the sky
so light dumped out like blood from a leak.
The boy in the trunk wouldn't die.

They drove and drove, and he dented the trunk's tight lid,
called their names, then pounded the wheel wells
with a tire iron. The sun filled
their skulls so they felt like hell

and the boy in the trunk wouldn't listen. You'd think
it was burning hot in there, you'd think he'd be gone,
passive, but no. The boy in the trunk
banged on and on

until the noise grew godalmighty unforgivable
and they had no choice but to pull into the woods,
leave the car, try to hitch a ride with someone
quieter, someone who could

listen without interrupting. They'd had a hot day.
The road simmered to the overheated sky.
But from far away they still heard him, the boy
in the trunk, his empty cry.

CHELSEA RATHBURN

Teaching Poetry at the School for the Blind

Their struggle to meet the image in the dark
is one we know — the storms, the hesitation —
but the shifting bridge they walk between idea
and braille's brief physical translation

reveals the sometimes lightness of our thoughts,
our casual groping for a better word,
as easy, slight as calling to our love
or remembering the chorus of a song we heard.

CHELSEA RATHBURN

Unused Lines

While words we pamper and protect
march off in search of meager fame,
these lines like bastard kids collect,
skulking through our notes in shame,

the discards of our intellect,
false starts, limp rhymes, feet bruised and lame,
condemned to suffer in neglect,
half-breeds that we refuse to name

for fear they'll prove what we suspect:
the damned and saved are much the same.

SUSAN RICH

———

December Journal Entry

Perhaps consider poetry
a gourmet grocery shop,

endless pyramids of
shape-shifting fruit:

persimmon, star flower, pomegranate —

and across the aisle
in hand-woven oval baskets:

Vietnamese coriander,
Thai basil, Chinese leaves.

Experiment without knowing
the exact region where

the pomegranate is grown
the pronunciation of the Chinese leaf.

But don't set out to deceive
the check-out girl;

you can't pretend that you're
a kumquat or a chanterelle.

And get away with it.

Instead, practice rapture —
and inquisitiveness, pose

a question to the golden
beet, the artichoke heart;

engage with a yellow fin.
The page relies

on the clean attempt
to move beyond the safe way.

Where is the ineffable?

Bring home a mango
prepare it with Kosher salt.

CYNTHIA NITZ RIS

Ghazal

*A poem should not mean
But be.*
— *Archibald MacLeish, "Ars Poetica"*

My life an open book, or so it seems
Yet, I can't even read the words, the seams

Unravel — it sounds like a command
A suave magician makes to silks that seem

Inert one moment, then alive with hope;
Blue infant whose chest expands now seems

Like Lazarus. More than a ghost — a man
Who first must leave this world before he seems

To know life, to see in brittle winter
Grass, the spring, or in the rock shelf, the seam

Of ore, the nugget of gold in mines
That bit by bit becomes the load, the seam

The horse struggles under, up winding paths
The prospector rides asleep; he seems

To dream of barrooms and clean chaps, whiskey,
Smooth skin — it won't last, but for now it seems

All is possibility, the world not
An oyster but fresh pearls. All things gleam, seem

Priceless, rare: the way you read me like
A book — the words and pages, even seams

Fascinate, and Cynthia's the moon in
Woman's form, with each compare more *is* than *seems.*

KIM ROBERTS

Mr. Jones Makes Poetry

Based on a painting of the same name by
Raoul Hausmann, 1920

With your coffee grinder and your vacant
blue stare, you look almost human,
Mr. Jones, almost capable of desire.

On the table, a green cylinder
calibrates the span of your palm,
a reassuring gesture of precision,

while the armless mannequin
is an extra body, should yours wear out
or lose the power to produce combustible words.

The mannequin has a knob instead of a head.
It stands ready to stand in, an understudy,
while each side of your symmetrical

mustache, Mr. Jones, mirrors the curve
of the coffee grinder's handle.
When cranked, the mustache moves on invisible gears,

each side alternates up and down like a piston,
and produces heat,
something actually alive.

Poets' Park, Mexico DF

You and I risked our necks to get there, dodging
the mad cars careening around it, merging
from all angles, a condensing asteroid
swarm. Our eyes, forced open, wept in the acrid
air. Breathlessly we landed on that island
green as imagination, nearly blind
to traffic, though we heard the autos grumble.
Throughout this miniature oasis people
strolled, played with their kids, lunched. One couple necked
like no tomorrow near a less romantic
memorial to a poet I'd never heard
of. His bronze head, looking grotesquely severed,
rested on an open concrete book
as if admonishing all poets, "Look
on this life, this work, and think again:
would you choose loving under this lush green
or locking yourself up in an attic room?
The real, polluted thing? Or some daydream?"
We walked arm in arm; head after bronze head
would neither speak nor smile nor grudge a nod.
Exhilaration? Gray contentment? Anguish?
Who knew? I had no syllable of Spanish.
Emerging from the poets' sanctuary,
the car-stink stinging, our eyes again gone blurry,
we found a fountain fashioned like a pen,
its nib replenishing a pool. A fountain-
pen. I pose beside it in your photo,
writing, writing forever with clear water.

JAY ROGOFF

A Breakdown

A.R. Ammons, 1926 - 2001

Coming from anywhere, your poems, they traveled
anywhere, rucksack on the back, hitching
up dungarees, hitching a ride, sentencing
down the road, letting their hair down, letting
themselves tumble down scroll-like and pushing
their lines through all those colons, never flinching
from all the nonsense we push through our colons,
compost being our biodegradable
identity, giving away the game,
giving off heady perfumes, signaling
hey, all the crap we spin out of ourselves:
haute cuisine for someone else, a fly, say, or
bacteria, imagination just
another enzyme, how the whole damned process
of breaking down never breaks down, whoa, never
ends, only that in the localest terms
we end, ending up brokedown into spelling
and if we're lucky intimations of
some glory and some end that we use to
distract us from that glory and that end.

KATE SCHAPIRA

The Fling

Instead of handing a poem to my parents, I hand
an excuse. Instead of making poems, I make headway.
Any visit I make I examine for poems
minutely, as for lice. Also any list. In laying
out my armor, breastplate and creases for next
morning, I'm layering and compressing
poems for later, the most possible, folded
or caught anywhere — "What's great
about poetry is it doesn't have to stop
there," my student said, I'm stealing it,
flocks of poems gather and yap over the roofs. Let's
say everyone you wanted to sleep with would have you
and it's up to you to conduct yourself
ecstatically, fairly — you'd prepare to say what you want.

BARRY SCHWABSKY

On Reverdy Road

They like poetry that isn't.
Not the kind that wakes into you
the way eyes gleam candid

in shadow, untrimmed wicks,
or that you grab from casual breezes
barehanded at dawn. When

don't the words in a poem
count? When they fall into a pit
and Dear Reader goes tumbling after.

DEREK SHEFFIELD

The Poem I Like Best

makes as much sense as a hunk of stone
warm enough to keep you
on your back, arms wide, eyes closed
long after the sun has moved on.

Ars Poetica: Married Version

A white chip of moon rules the sky
        as I pad softly across the driveway,
open the door of my house, and step in.
        Weaving through whisking thumps
of the dog's tail, scattered crayons
        and dolls, I make my way
past the door of my daughter's room,
        and into the kitchen where the coffee maker
is making its final gurgles. I pour a hot cup,
        add cream, and stir. From here,
at this early hour, my study is no longer
        a garage. Its lighted window
looks more like the back of a bronze chariot
        drawn by winged, see-through horses,
and that pulsing drone is an echo
        of a distant horn, and not the refrigerator.
Is that what she sees from this vantage at the sink
        when I am writing and framed in that light?
Am I a clever, leaf-crowned god stroking his beard
        and stitching the void with electric lines?
Or, as she's scrubbing dried egg
        from a plate, twisting a can opener,
does she see something else? A beast, perhaps,
        obsessed with writhing every morning
in its own shit, hairy, helpless, and beyond itself
        under the great and glowing bone in the sky?

SHOSHAUNA SHY

A Poet's Winter

No poem stalks me
so I start the chase: Eavesdrop
on children, walk abandoned houses,
wear my uncle's sweatshirt, read
Newsweek backwards.
In exhaustion I surrender
to the suction of sleep.
Whispering together
in the rafters above me,
crystal-bright sestinas
drift down like snowflakes,
giggle on contact,
then dissolve.

White Poem

Poems
crop up in my mouth
like baby teeth

It will take
one night sleeping alone
in a white room
to jar them loose

Stone Soup

Though I use words,
make from
and by words,
words are neither my clay
or my wheel,
my pot nor my spuds.
Words
are commonplace,
even in poverty
there are too many of them.

Pinch of salt,
pinch a rhyme —
it's forgers and spinners
call language a 'tool'.
And to call it a 'craft'
suggests
too set a goal
too honed a procedure.

Surely,
the poetic trick is
making a meal from
the saucepan.

―

ordinary poet

tongue world can be tongue for the poet and
poetry is hallo everywhere hallo all everywhere poetry all
everywhere so the poet lets place for instant collages
dumb poems express poems visual poetry found mixed poems

poetry feeds on everything hallo hallo everything that created
his existence readings relationships coarse expressions wet & sweet
dreams songs physical activities constructions travels reflections
contemplations food
primary ordinary elementary this a primary ordinary elementary
poetry

when someone is asking questions what is poetry today
which date how old how many why he answers
"poetry today is when I say it is poetry"
he is a poet when doing what he says
he is the tree and the spade cutting roots
he is the kid's hand in the grit stoop
he is the nail scrap deep in dog's belly
he is the flax stem dripping in the river
brown water while shells are falling over the forest
an ice-blink in a mirror-wardrobe grinning door

poetry is coming from the greedy emptiness vibrating in
the corporeal pipe yes that is the superficial envelope
of this tube it accepts scrap friction aggression information
caress noise & smell minimal cosmos infinite as infinity

he is an ordinary poet using his brain breath
and body brain and breath breath brain and body
the poet and the publisher live together in him
like the gardener and the weary reader live together
in him like the translator and the father live
together in him like the merz and the chess
player live together in him like the stunted brain
and the knotted bowels live together in him like
the vertebras and the thigh bones live together in

him like the liver and the nasal mucus live
together in him like the hardhitter and the quinquagenerian
live together in him like the guitar player and
the microbe live together in him like the beerdrinker
and the veal chop live together in him like
the starscrewer and the snail live together in him
like the waste and the memory holes live together
in him like the rider and the salad live
together in him like this like this and still
like this his body brain and breath and body

ROD SUMMERS

New Hazards

25/04/2005 14:33

The Blackbird;
Within whose territory I garden,
Has a brown wife and daughter.
His son, long gone, was driven out again
When testosterone rose, regular as sap, this Spring ...
A tiny fly circumnavigates my spectacles
And, attracted by my sparkling teardrops,
Drowns itself in my eye,
Leaving me it's pain & residue.
Fucking nature! Who needs it?
End of poem

Taking a break from filing books
Out of poets into the computer
To tea and an hour's deep thought
About the books I read
And the books V.B. reads
And how healthy it is to have an obsession
(Unless it's picking scabs.)
Rock & Roll, Egil & Njall
Sharing a cloud with Rory
Books that glow in the dark stone
Illuminated instruction.
The courageous spirit of the imagination
Game - set and disposable lighter
One man's obscure is also his reality.
Shit! I let my tea go cold
Back to the scree

25/04/2005 16:12
r.s.s.
maastricht

EILEEN TABIOS

—————

Athena

What's deemed necessary
changes. Hear
me

listening in another
decade, editing
last

and first lines.
A different
Singer

croons from behind
an impassive
speaker.

I listen, cross
out more
lines.

The poem cannot
be pure.
Sound

never travels unimpeded
by anonymous
butterflies.

Writing it down
merely freezes
flight —

Translation: an inevitable
fall. Take
control

by shooting it
as if
pigeons

were clay: This
one is.
But

It provided pleasure
once, was
"necessary."

Once, it flew
with non-imaginary
wings.

O, clay pigeon.
Translation: the
error

is my ear's.
The sky
ruptured

suddenly — I saw
but did
not

hear the precursor
fall of
leaves.

*****

Edit it down.
Edit it
down.

Silence is Queen,
not lady
-in-waiting.

Edit it down.
Edit it.
Edit

it down. Edit
it. Edit.
Edit.

Ars Poetica

Poetry is the devil's footprint,
the hummingbird's needle.
It's how you may outlive your life.

The first words stir
like the fanfare of the elevator, then
are swallowed up in the confusion of arrival.

You let down your guard, you've brought
only as much memory as you'll need.

You're listening for the cries of gulls,
your mother's voice,
the directives of the wind

as there, crashing toward shore,
the pieces of ocean
reattach in the oncoming wave.

Poetry is where you were headed
while the world was pointing
in the opposite direction.

Poetry is a word that requires no reply,
a catalogue of itch, pain, air-hunger.
By means of it, you sense hatred
or the need to be touched.

For most of its existence
it is folded neatly inside the brain,
in the part that makes us believe
we are human.

HEATHER THOMAS

Awakening

you are not your mind you are not your mind you are not

       the poem is
       not your body

is language an ocean we live   coming to
          forms   proof
             she was coming to

blank space where the body could be blank space

      wave
         curve   ink
            jet

        wet   wide   open

thought lands wild   (grief is simple and dark)

      hard
         to turn
      away

turn into the one you want or each next enter the split

      mount an enormous
            struggle
     with fictions
         enormous
rushing past

  will you be close

       calm

   utterly solitude

utterly
　　　maple, moss

my plot is marvelous this fine gauze

　　　conceals　　　practices

hard careful digging hard careful digging hard

　　　cold part
　　　　who

　　would imagine

　　　life like
　　　　　words

DAVID TIPTON

Rejection: A Small Ars Poetica, Sort Of

"Though the manuscript you sent has not found a place with us ...
— The Editors"

Well, here's another one. And like the others before it (are they
folding-out siblings or mere carbon copies?), it's dressed in nice
finery, with shadowy chain-lines running throughout — just like the
ones in our elegant stationary or in elderly tomes, so believable. —
And how we believed it, believe me, and so rightly feared,

shaking inside our booths before its austerity and the well
structured speeches it always pulled out of its inside vest pocket
and read out like a sentence artfully spooled in a single paragraph
working smoothly as plumbing, which left us so weakened, like
those lead dreams of our youth. But we're so far

past it now, taking it as no more than a commercial thing — like
those worn PSAs that accuse us and warn us — and so address it by
leaving chocolate cookies on the coffee table for whenever it may
next arrive: snacks we dispense as glib tokens. But recently, there's
this interesting spin-off: A maddening drive

to write a history of things as they are — something I do in closed
quarters, pretending the mercury-vapor light is a kerosene lamp
whose smoky chimney sends out a burnt oily smell. — I think
that's why the tight lines keep breaking in odd places before
reaching the right margin, depicting you as a fair damsel

chained by love inside an ogre's keepsake box; and me a sad
crowbar bent in night light in the effort and hope of actually
prying you out.

JUANITA TORRENCE-THOMPSON

Poetry Is ... (A Sestina)

Oh blue-green poetry
master of pithy words,
sometimes thy name is reality
gliding through war-torn streets of life
wandering through deserts, scaling mountain peaks
or luxuriating in a sphere of fantasy

But why create fantasy
with iridescent poetry
of angels, dragons and gnomes atop peaks
The essence of magical words
When the richness of life
Lies before you to pluck its reality

But what is reality
Yours may be his fantasy
sans all the rules of life
which can be culled in poetry
Choosing the right words
are paramount, so your verse can peak

Of course some peaks
rise higher than others. Reality
is king for a while, basking in truthful words
shoving all imaginative fantasies
aside, marching triumphantly through poetry
— the manna of life.

But many things depict life.
Some do reach the highest peaks
through air-borne poetry,
while others seek truth in reality.
Still others debunk fantasy
reveling in ascerbic words.

But thoughts can be written words,
and can make or break a life,
steer one toward childlike fantasy
and soar eagle-like over peaks,
thumbing your nose at reality
through satiny elastic language of poetry.

Whatever your words, make them peak.
Scour through life. Find your truth, your reality.
Not the fantasy. Make it your poetry.

Poetry 301

The antique clock
chimes past her breakfast
of pancakes, Canadian bacon
and lunch of Caesar salad

The page is still blank
blank as a poker player
as the still air cuts her
like a machete
deeply wounding her psyche

The silence washes over her
searing her senses
like drizzled olive oil
over wild salmon

As the chiming clock sings six
she savors spinach, asparagus
salad and sea bass

When the clock chimes seven
her fingers fly to heaven
Her computer is alive
with words, words, words
toppling over each other,
expanding and bursting
into lines, stanzas, pages
crafting into free verse,
sestinas, villanelles
as she writes into the night
sipping Red Zinger tea.

WILLIAM TROWBRIDGE

New New Formalist

The giveaway's the eyes: no real elan,
apologetic, the focus out of whack
as I pedal onto the wire to show I can

compose a villanelle, like anyone
who, through with nets and tethers, has the knack,
whose eyes should wellneigh radiate elan

despite the skimpy audience's deadpan
stare, who's finally able to attack
the line the uninitiated doubt they can.

"There's better music in a broken fan,"
I hear old timers sigh, jarring me back
to where my eyes bleared from low elan,

when I lost balance and a quarter of my tan.
I'm breathing hard, confronted with my lack
of poise on the wire, trying to show I can

prevail when shit's inquiring after fan.
I'm almost there, dear friend; don't turn your back:
just watch them film me now, pumping with elan,
wired on closure, this beauty in the can.

PRISCILA UPPAL

careful careful

if you drop this poem
it won't forgive you
won't return even one
of your calls it will
pass you by on the street
looking the other way
with shades on and heeled
shoes and never will it
trust you again or lie
in your arms or care if
you cry or even stop to
watch you fall it has no
time for you if you can't
hold for just a second
wait for it to adjust
to the bumps in your hands
remember if you drop this
poem with certainty
it will never admit it
ever loved you, not to anyone

Priscila Uppal

Sometimes I'm Not Sure I Agree
with What I Write

Sometimes I'm not sure I agree with what I write,
if the air I breathe is really and truly stale and bland
in the basement. If you have a pointed nose
like a bird's beak or eyes the shade of burnt sunflowers.
I'm at a loss as to whether our house has Victorian trim
around the windows or an art-deco kitchen, and no one's
confirmed to my satisfaction that the door handle
jiggles because of that awful winter in 1995.

Is my father actually to be pitied?
My mother mythologized?
My version of my lost childhood anthologized?

I've got the sad thing down like a posture.
The weeping willows roll in when called.
The death warrants stack themselves paper upon
paper, never caught in the printer.

Sorrow is no longer unexpected. It arrives
with every breath and bird's beak and door handle. Winter
or summer, that awful feeling of it being there
whether it's already left or not.

KATHRINE VARNES

Folding the Laundry I Think About Aesthetics

And the conventions of this poem, for instance,
the meditation pinned against the domestic
as the sleeves against the tee shirt shoulder blades

that never fit quite right but we cram
into a drawer anyway. The way slightly damp
cotton of flannel sheets should bring me

to irresistible truth, the coming together
and parting of two people holding the corners,
when in fact I fold most of our sheets by myself

in a hurried haphazard motion on the newly
cleaned carpet or bed, since he slows me down
with twisting his end in the play of an anti-folder.

I do not smile, except always on accident, to myself,
which is his favorite. Do you really want to hear
about his boxer shorts? Or what I think about them?

We could make them stand for just about anything, you and I,
or consider the sock wadded up in the pillowcase,
the tilting pile of clean laundry on the chair

onto which I will add this listing tower
of like put next to like for easy stowing.
It would be easy to fill each item with body,

mention the socks rolled into pairs that keep
their knees together, the bras that dry in the open air
no matter what anyone says and work it into a metaphor

of love and life together, a dream of the ordinary
poem that makes some laundry magic again
if not particularly moral or worthy of praise.

JEANNE WAGNER

Poems

shouldn't be read out loud.
They should be written in solitude,
the paper folded into small squares,
plain side out, then passed in secret
like billets doux
carried around all day
buried inside warm pockets,
pressed against thigh and groin.
Their powers of seduction
so private,
biblical injunctions
leap to mind.

They should be denounced
from the pulpit,
debated on talk shows,
those who write them
subjected to lengthy screening
at airports and borders.

They should be preserved
in a lost language,
the key to deciphering it,
another language lost
to all but a few,

both inscribed
on a hard black stone
with a name like a small flower,
to remind us how encrypted
beauty is,
forced up from rootstock,
and tongue-tied bud.

JEANNE WAGNER

Ars Poetica

Sometimes I think of Shelley's heart,
which was finally buried,
but there was that hour on the beach
when his friends worked, so inexpertly,
to build a funeral pyre:
struggling with the wind
and the wrong kind of kindling,
with the wet exhumation of his body
from the waves;

suffering from the stench,
and the smoke, and the way,
even after his body was consumed by fire,
the horrible sac of the heart still held out,
gorged on heat,
scorching the hand that reached out for it,
refusing to burn.

AMY WATKINS

What I Love About Fiction

Turning each page, how fast
they pile up in your left hand,
how your progress is marked
by a bookmark's steady march
through leaves. And poetry, the opposite:
how slowly you move from poem
to poem, how long it takes
to read one slender volume,
how each night you turn only one
or two pages, carefully,
and then sleep,
like learning to love a skinny
and complicated girl.

AMY WATKINS

When I Am Asked

When I am asked
how I began writing poems,
I talk about the indifference of nature
— Lisel Mueller

When I am asked
how I began writing poems,
I talk about my father's bruised
thumbnail, how my father, grandfather
and uncles, carpenters all,
stride the bare trusses of my childhood
in cracked work boots, each
with one ridged fingernail turning
purple then black then yellow forever.
They are building our home again
out of things that can hurt them —
concrete blocks and rough wood
and nails longer than my fingers.

My mother collects all the dropped
nails and shingles, singing hymns
and John Denver songs.

For You/New Psalm

we have
language
native
as it is
for us
untaught
in, of, from
life itself
directly
from us
for us
as it is.

we have it too, too obviously,
slimy institutional
school of stagnation
mass word
lifelessness
so many fingered.

things fresh and alive
the way they are
pointing
through blockage
things clear all over
a poem

a tree
or pool of tide, for a while
that grows
what it means to be
word-life,
poem, home

Poetics

The poets tell me things like *Hooray for refuse.* Like, *There's a grackle in the crotch of that tree.* The poets freak me out. I hide from them by posing as a tree. I stand in tree posture, on one leg, arms in a diamond above my head.

Tree posture does not so much look like a tree as a cartoon Egyptian, but the poets don't know the difference.

Something in the poets is broken.

The problem with the poets is that they will just stand there staring at me, thinking I am a tree. They will stand there all day. The poets never get bored. A grackle will land on my crotch and rest there, and then the poets will stare at the grackle. They will look at the grackle's black feathers and see purple feathers and red feathers and blue feathers and green feathers. They will see themselves reflected in the feathers' oily shine. When the grackle flies off, they will sit down in the shade beneath me and pluck their lutes and hum. If they fall asleep I can sneak away, but I usually have to wait until they get hungry or thirsty or shivery. This can take hours or days.

I try to avoid the poets, to duck around a corner or into a store before they see me, but I do not always see them coming. Sometimes I am taken by surprise.

CAROL CLARK WILLIAMS

Chain Poem

Important! Read carefully!
Do not disregard
this message — It is real.
When you receive this poem,
open your mind.
Write down seven thoughts
expressed as mental pictures.
(These thoughts can be on any subject:
politics and sorrow, love
and sorrow, life and sorrow ...)
Do not discard this poem
or terrible things will happen:
Ideas will be abandoned unexpressed,
love will not be spoken,
a concrete image will dissolve in tears.
A man in Alabama received this poem:
within twenty-four hours of reading it,
his blindness had been lifted.
A woman in New Jersey got this poem:
within one week of reading it, she began
a journal which clarified her life.
You, too, can use this poem
to your good fortune. Here is how:
Express an idea concisely and beautifully
as you can. Write a title at the top of the page.
At the bottom, sign your name preceded by
a small, circled "c" and the date.
Read it aloud to five of your best-loved friends.
Wait for results to follow.

CAROL CLARK WILLIAMS

Poetry Lover

Eventually it stalks
the chantry of your mind
with heavy step and a proud face,
sits at your communion table,
fork and knife poised in its hands,
criticizes the elements and their presentation,
becomes the Adversary.

Eventually it demands
both sides of the bed,
total control of the television remote,
dictates what music
you can play on the stereo,
takes over the closet.

Far cry from the day
it knocked timidly
on your half-open door,
knelt at your feet,
waiting to speak. Or fled,
and you eagerly pursued it
down the merciless streets.

The Fifth Day

I spent five days enraptured
An established poet
signing his book of poetry
had written 'to Jacquie
fellow poet, with respect.'
I was lifted to a pleasant wonder
and showed it to all I met.
Enjoying, each time, the compliment.
Most said 'that was nice of him'
on the fifth day
Jenny with clear honest eyes
Said 'Why wouldn't he?'
Didn't she understand?
No she was moving me on
to acceptance,
to a higher wonder
I am a poet. (How hard to write).

JACQUIE WILLIAMS

About Poetry

I just want to tell you about poetry
because I don't really know what it is
Mr Ramsbottom my teacher said it was
stuff that rhymed,
had verses
and it was neat and tidy
we used to learn
daffodils and
I must go down to the sea again
to the lonely sea and the sky
and that sort of thing
they don't write poetry like that any more

now they can stand up and say two words
and it's a poem
it's a real good poem
you have to know which 2 words to say though
and you have to say them right
so that people know it's a poem

any how
for something to do
I've written you a poem

Birds sing in sky
My brain flys by
wondering why
we live and die

that poem had 14 words

"The Man Is Only Half Himself, the Other Half Is His Expression"

— *Ralph Waldo Emerson*

Driven from hearth and home
by the appetite of the seeker for the sea,
the poem set out to find itself
its place, its nightmare, its fable
the love of its life
its epigram, its pantoumness
villanelleness, Shakespearean and
Petrarchian sonnetness
its Keats oatmeal
its Dante Beatrice, its Whitman mammoth
its reverent Rumi ribald.

It searches academia
bars, cafes, Poets House, City Lights
the Library of Congress Poetry at Midnight
Mecca, the Louvre
the Serengetti
and finally descends into hell
rising on the third day
it can't face heaven
(what if there is none)
takes a chance on the moon
in all its gibbousness —
hello, the moon is full of luminous things
nonsense, mimsy, legend
has a metaphorical nose
eyes made of similes
similes made of smiles
and a tongue that says this:

Home is where the hearth is
the poet is there in a purple velvet chair
holding a silver pen
barely touching the parchment

waiting to bestow grace and beauty
waiting to warm you
ready to bring you from the fire
ready to write you wild in the world
ready to let you go.

ERNIE WORMWOOD

———

Ars Poetica

We are changing this world
one poem at a time
I the writer and you the listener.

                    Quiet now.

Do you hear me reading it to you?
Do you see me leaping from the page
to hold your ear wide open as I whisper
my poem or shout my poem or simply
let the poem out of my body into yours?
You are different as soon as you hear it.
I am different as soon as you hear it,

                    even in death.

No matter how many there were before me,
you are a virgin to my poem and my poem is hot for you,
my poem wants you more than anything,
my poem is the slut of the century for sure.

MARK YOUNG

Keeping my hand in

Residual traces of the
lightning strikes
linger on the surface
of the optic nerves. Some
might see paintings
in them, or sculptures
carved from the Carrera marble
that Michelangelo loved
so much. Others
will attach visions, talk
of pathways to the world
beyond, flood-lit avenues
or lights at the end of
tunnels. The poet, prosaic,
counts the time until
the thunder arrives.

Mark Young

Text
or text-
ure. The feel

of
words as
you push them

into
place. Braille
for the eye.

ANDRENA ZAWINSKI

—————

The Poet Driving

The poet,
white knuckled
at the podium, drives
the crowd. And reeling,
as if taking on mountainous S curves,
or hydroplaning minefields,
the poet maps metaphors
in shag bark and hickory, staggering
the dappled sundown.

This could be
Kansas, Saigon, Mozambique, Peoria,
a road, bridge, underpass
where the poet dresses deathbeds
in thin sheets
of memory.
The clenched fist
becomes an open hand,
fingers that point
press into prayer.

And our silences
grow ravenous for this.
We choke down whole landscapes,
drink in cloud bursts, throb
with the starlit sky. We lean into the words
like a slow dance pinned to ourselves
like a corsage, like a lover, like a poem,
like the language
of applause.

ANDRENA ZAWINSKI

Writing Lesson

" ... all they want to do
is tie the poem to a chair with rope
and torture a confession out of it ... "

— Introduction to Poetry, by Billy Collins

You knew you were in trouble
the second you put the plate on the table —
those sesame snow peas and truffles
you drizzled with kumquat and ginger
to impress your poetry potluck writing group —
when he said, Not Chinese again.

You knew you were in-for-it
when he called your poem a travelogue of Paris
grinding down the wrong track
with its Kunitz epigraph fumbling at the gears
as he blasted, The old man got to wear
that crown of Laureate just for his age.

You knew, despite your mince and trim
and folding in its metaphoric light,
this poem would be tied to the chair
with a rope, have the life beaten from it,
a flabby bunch of bunkum flattened
with his belting, Where is the cri de coeur?

And you knew in the way you know
in a half-wake state when you hear a train
in the distance barreling into your sleep
in a blur of whistles and grinds and whirs,
its metal scraping rails in a still night, deep
in dark, its muffled blue note wailing.

You knew you must be dreaming this
standing before a train coming on headlong
at you half-naked there, a train about to slice

through what you peeled down to —
an awful tutu, mismatched shoes, feather cloche
you shouldn't be caught dead in.

Then this man with a train for a mouth
tells you this is not a well-lit poem
and the guy donning laurels in the first car
misdirected it — that it's rocketing
down the wrong track on a collision course
headed right for Gare du Nord.

And you actually thank this man, talking
with a mouthful of train, for his observation.
But you don't write a word for days
then weeks as you focus instead your eyes
on a wind riding dunes hitched to a slice
of tangerine light, shapeshifting sunset.

You put your ear to the movement of earth
beneath a frenzy of shorebirds pecking the eyes
from a head of a beached seal there. And speechless,
you listen for a fading blue note of a train
in the distance, off to somewhere far away.

NOTES & CREDITS

———

KELLI RUSSELL AGODON is the author of *Small Knots* and the chapbook, *Geography*. She is the Co-Editor of Crab Creek Review. Visit her webpage at: www.agodon.com

FLOR AGUILERA GARCIA (Mexico City) is a film critic and fiction writer. Her poetry books include: *Last Flight to Shanghai* (Praxis, 2002), *55 frames per second* (Praxis, 2005), *Butoh* (Tintanueva, 2008) and *As the Audience Begs for a Ferocious Tango* (San Francisco Bay Press, 2009).

KARREN LALONDE ALIENIER is author of *Looking for Divine Transportation*, winner of the 2002 Towson University Prize for Literature, and *The Steiny Road to Operadom: The Making of American Operas*. She writes for *Scene4 Magazine*. More information at alenier.blogspot.com.

SANDRA ALLAND is a writer and multimedia artist. She's currently an artist-in-residence at Glasgow Gallery of Modern Art, and works with the poetry-music fusion band, *Zorras*. She has published two books of poetry and a slew of chapbooks. Find out more at www.blissfultimes.ca

C. J. ALLEN's poetry has appeared in a wide range of magazines (from *Poetry Review* to *Modern Painters*) and anthologies in the UK & Ireland, and has been broadcast on BBC Radios 3 & 4. He is the author of four collections of poems, most recently *A Strange Arrangement: New & Collected Poems*, from Leafe Press (www.leafepress.com).

IVAN ARGUELLES is the author of numerous poetry collections, notably: *The Invention of Spain, Looking for Mary Lou* (William Carlos Williams Award, 1989), *"That" Goddess*, and *Madonna Septet* (2 vols.). He is founder and co-editor of Pantograph Press.

ANNY BALLARDINI received her MFA in Creative
Writing from UNO, Uni of New Orleans. She teaches
high school; edits *Poets' Corner*, and writes a blog:
Narcissus Works. Her two poetry collections are:
Opening and Closing Numbers (2005), and *Ghost
Dance in 33 Movements* (2009).

GARY BARWIN's many books include the chapbooks
Inverting the Deer, Punctuation Funnies, and *anus
porcupine eyebrow*. A new book is forthcoming from
Coach House. He lives in Hamilton, Ontario and can
be found at serifofnottingham.blogspot.com.

ANNETTE BASALYGA has received a Duncan Lawrie Prize
and also a grant from the Pennsylvania Council on the
Arts. She was resident poet at the Island Institute in
Sitka, Alaska, and in April, a guest poet at The Robert
Frost Poetry Festival in Key West, Florida.

RICK BENJAMIN teaches poetry & community practice at
Brown University & the Rhode Island School of
Design, and is also on the faculty of the MFA program
in Interdisciplinary Arts at Goddard College. His book
of poems, *Passing Love*, is forthcoming from Wolf
Ridge Press.

JOHN M. BENNETT has published over 300 books and
chapbooks of poetry, visual poetry, collaborations,
scholarly works, and other materials. He is Curator
of the *Avant Writing Collection* at The Ohio State
University. He has performed and exhibited his work
worldwide.

MAXIANNE BERGER's most recent book is *Dismantled
Secrets* (Wolsak and Wynn, 2008). She likes to play
with form, from haiku through nonce to OuliPo-ish
abecedarians and paradelles. When not poeming,
she is an audiologist at the McGill University Health
Centre.

F. J. BERGMANN frequents Wisconsin and fibitz.com.
Her work has appeared in *Asimov's, MARGIE, Opium,
Southern Poetry Review, Weird Tales*, and her most
recent chapbook, *Constellation of the Dragonfly* (Plan
B Press, 2008). Her hairstyle is deceptive.

CLIFF BERNIER'S chapbook *Earth Suite* is forthcoming from Finishing Line Press. A second chapbook, *Dark Berries*, is forthcoming from Pudding House Publications. He has been nominated for a Pushcart Prize and a Best of the Net Award.

GREGORY BETTS is the author of *If Language, Haikube*, and the forthcoming *The Others Raisd in Me* (Pedlar Press, Fall 2009). He lives in St. Catharines where he teaches Avant-Garde and Canadian Literature at Brock University. For more, check out epc.buffalo.edu/authors/betts

CELIA BLAND is the author of *Soft Box*, a collection of poetry. She has published recently in *Writing on the Edge, The Boston Review, The Valparaiso Poetry Review* and *Poets & Writers*. She teaches at Bard College.

DEAN BLEHERT'S poems appear at www.blehert.com. He has seven books out, including *Please, Lord, Make Me A Famous Poet Or At Least Less Fat*. He emails a short poem daily to 2500. Contact him through his website to get on his email list.

HELEN BOETTCHER was born in Aigion, Greece, but grew up in Melbourne, Australia. Her first poem was written when she was nine years old. The next poem found its way on paper more than forty years later. She likes to dwell on things.

PETER BOYLE is not the actor, but Peter Boyle the Australian poet. He began writing poetry at age 15 but had his first book, *Coming home from the world*, published at age 43. His most recent book *Apocrypha* (Vagabond Press, 2009) interweaves poetry and short poetic fictions.

ALLEN BRADEN of Lakewood, Washington, has poetry anthologized in *Best New Poets, Spreading the Word: Editors on Poetry, Poets of the American West* and several literature textbooks. His book of poems is *A Wreath of Down and Drops of Blood* (University of Georgia Press, 2010).

THERESE L. BRODERICK resides in Albany, NY, with her husband and teenage daughter. She is a longtime member of the minority Soccer Mom school of poets. To find out more about her poetry activities, publications, and awards, visit http://theresebroderick.wordpress.com.

MARY BUCHINGER's poems have appeared in *Cortland Review, RUNES, The Massachusetts Review, Versal,* and other journals. She holds a Ph.D. in linguistics and teaches writing and communication studies at the Massachusetts College of Pharmacy and Health Sciences in Boston.

ANA BUIGUES does a lot of things and lives in the wonderful world of ideas. She has several degrees in art history from the University of Valencia and The University of Toronto. Whether getting these degrees was a useful thing to do is still being investigated.

MIKE BURWELL writes environmental impact statements, maintains a shipwreck database for Alaska, and teaches poetry part-time at the University of Alaska Anchorage. His first full-length poetry collection, *Cartography of Water,* was published in December 2007 by NorthShore Press.

MAIRÉAD BYRNE's collections include *Talk Poetry* (Miami University Press, 2007), *SOS Poetry* (/ubu Editions, 2007) and *Nelson & The Huruburu Bird* (Wild Honey Press 2003). A Dubliner, she hosts a reading/performance series in Providence, *couscous@tazza*—actually a movable feast.

NICK CARBÓ is the author of four books of poetry, the latest being *Chinese, Japanese, What are These?* (Pecan Grove Press, 2009). He has won NEA and NYFA grants and his film poems have been premiered in Bury, U.K. & Manila, Philippines.

CATHY CARLISI's writing has appeared in the *Prairie Schooner, The Mid-American Review, Rhino, The Southern Poetry Review, The Atlanta Review* and others. She is the Chief Creative Officer at Brighthouse in Atlanta.

WENDY TAYLOR CARLISLE lives on the edge of Texas. She is the author of two books, *Reading Berryman to the Dog* (2000), *Discount Fireworks* (2008), and two chapbooks, *After Happily Ever*, and *The Storage of Angels*. Find more about her at http://www.wendytaylorcarlisle.com

JAMES CERVANTES' fourth book of poetry, *Temporary Meaning*, was nominated for a Los Angeles Times book award in poetry in 2007. Cervantes, also editor of the online journal, *The Salt River Review*, now divides his time between Arizona and San Miguel de Allende.

JOEL CHACE has had work in magazines such as *6ix*, *xStream*, *Three Candles*, and *Jacket*. He has published more than a dozen collections: matter no matter (Paper Kite Press, 2008), A Script (Otoliths Books); and many others. Chace is Poetry Editor for *5_trope*.

ELLEN ARONOFSKY COLE is a poet, actress, puppeteer, and teaching artist, as well as the mother of two wonderful girls and a baby parrot. Her publication credits include *The Potomac Review, Innisfree Poetry Journal, Bogg*, and *The Takoma Voice*.

ED COLETTI is also a painter, and has been writing poetry for over 45 years. After studying with Robert Creeley at San Francisco State University, he published numerous books and has contributed to a wide variety of national journals and anthologies. Ed lives in Santa Rosa, CA.

JENNIFER COMPTON lives in Australia and is a poet and playwright who also writes prose. Recently her poetry has been published in *Stand, Poetry London, Poetry New Zealand* and *Quadrant*. In 2010 she will be a guest at Sarajevo Poetry Days.

ANNE CORAY is the author of *Bone Strings* (Scarlet Tanager Books), *Soon the Wind* (Finishing Line Press); and coeditor of *Crosscurrents North: Alaskans on the Environment* (University of Alaska Press). She lives at her birthplace on remote Qizhjeh Vena in southwest Alaska.

ALISON CROGGON lives in Melbourne, Australia. Her most recent poetry collection is *Theatre* (Salt Publishing 2008). She is also a theatre critic and the author of the popular fantasy quartet The Books of Pellinor.

DEL RAY CROSS edits *Shampoo* (ShampooPoetry.com) and his books of poetry include *Luf Luffly* and *Cinema Yosemite* (Pressed Wafer) and *Ein frisches Trugbild* (Luxbooks, in English with German translations by Peter Rehberg, illustrations by Jessica McLeod).

CRAIG CZURY works as a poet in schools, homeless shelters, prisons, mental hospitals and community centers throughout the world. His books have been translated to Spanish, Russian, Lithuanian, Croatian, Albanian and Italian. He is the author of *Kitchen Of Conflict Resolution* and *American Know-how: Patent Pending*.

YOKO DANNO is Japanese. Her poetry books, *Trilogy* (1970), *Hagoromo* (1984), *Epitaph for Memories* (2004), are in English. *The Blue Door* (2006) and *A Sleeping Tiger Dreams of Manhattan* (2008) are co-written with James C. Hopkins. *Songs and Stories of the Kojiki* is a translation (2008).

LUCILLE LANG DAY is the author of eight poetry collections and chapbooks, including *The Curvature of Blue* (Cervena Barva, 2009) and *The Book of Answers* (Finishing Line, 2006). She has also published a children's book and is the founder and director of Scarlet Tanager Books.

DENISE DUHAMEL'S most recent poetry titles are *Ka-Ching!* (University of Pittsburgh Press, 2009); *Two and Two* (Pittsburgh, 2005); *Mille et un Sentiments* (Firewheel, 2005); and *Queen for a Day: Selected and New Poems* (Pittsburgh, 2001).

PATRICK JAMES DUNAGAN lives and works in San Francisco. His work has appeared in *Big Bell, Blue Book, Cannibal, Chain, Forklift, Morning Train, One Less Magazine,* and *Pompom*. Recent chapbooks: *From Chansonniers* (Blue Press, 2008), *Easy Eden with Micah Ballard* (PUSH, 2009).

RICCARDO DURANTI poet: also teacher, translator, gardener, photographer, olive oil producer. Four books and ten pamphlets of poems already published, in Italian, English and a local dialect spoken by a population of 500. One more, *Meditamondo*, ready, but no time to publish it.

PAUL DUTTON is a poet, novelist, essayist, musician, and oral sound artist. He has read and performed, solo and ensemble (the Four Horsemen, CCMC), throughout Europe and the Americas. Most recent works are *Several Women Dancing* (novel) and *Oralizations* (CD).

SUSANNE DYCKMAN'S work has appeared in a full-length volume, *equilibrium's form* (Shearsman Books), two chapbooks, *Counterweight* (Woodland Editions) and *Transiting Indigo* (EtherDome), and a number of journals. She is also host and curator of the Evelyn Avenue reading series.

LYNNELL EDWARDS is the author of two full-length collections of poetry: *The Farmer's Daughter* and *The Highwayman's Wife*, both from Red Hen Press. Her work has been twice-nominated for a Pushcart Prize. She lives in Louisville, Kentucky.

DAN FEATHERSTON'S books of poetry include *The Radiant World* (BlazeVox, 2009), *The Clock Maker's Memoir* (Cuneiform Press, 2007), and *United States* (Factory School, 2005). He lives in Philadelphia and teaches at Temple University.

ANNIE FINCH is author or editor of fifteen books, most recently *Calendars, Among the Goddesses: An Epic*, and *The Body of Poetry: Essays*. Her work was shortlisted for Foreword Poetry Book of the Year and won the Fitzgerald Award. She directs Stonecoast, the low-residency MFA.

THOMAS FINK is the author of five books of poetry, most recently *Clarity and Other Poems* (Marsh Hawk Press, 2008) and two books of criticism. His work appeared in the *Best American Poetry 2007*. Fink's paintings hang in various collections.

ALAN HALSEY'S recent books are *Lives of the Poets* (Five Seasons Press) and *Term as in Aftermath* (Ahadada Books). *Marginalien* (Five Seasons, 2005) collects his poems, prose & graphics 1988-2004, and *Not Everything Remotely* (Salt, 2006) is a selected poems 1978-2005.

SHARON HARRIS is "a woman of ethereal interests" (Toronto Life), the author of *Avatar* (The Mercury Press), the curator of iloveyougalleries.com and iloveyougraffiti.com, the blogger at theiloveyougblog.com, and a hockey player (#143). She loves you.

LOLA HASKINS' work includes poetry advice (*Not Feathers Yet*), fables about women (*Solutions Beginning with A*), and 8 books of poems, most lately a new and selected (*Desire Lines*). For more information, please see www.lolahaskins.com.

NELLIE HILL'S recent chapbook is *My Daily Walk* (Pudding House, 2008). She has an acupressure practice in Berkeley where she lives.

NATHAN HOKS has recently published poems in *Lungfull!, Bateau, Mrs. Maybe,* and *InDigest.* He holds an MFA and an MA from the University of Iowa. He lives in Somerville, Massachusetts, with his wife and son.

PAUL HOOVER has published twelve books of poetry including *Sonnet 56* (2009), *Edge and Fold* (2006), and *Poems in Spanish* (2005). He is editor of *Postmodern American Poetry: A Norton Anthology,* and, with Maxine Chernoff, the literary magazine, *New American Writing.*

MIKHAIL HOROWITZ is the author of *Big League Poets* (City Lights, 1978) and two books of poetry. His performance work has been featured on many CDs, including *The Blues of the Birth* (jazz fables; Sundazed Records).

RAY HSU is Postdoctoral Fellow in Creative Writing at UBC. His book, *Anthropy*, won the 2005 League of Canadian Poets' Gerald Lampert Award for best first book and was a finalist for the Trillium Book Award for Poetry.

HALVARD JOHNSON spends his quality time in San Miguel de Allende, Guanajuato, Mexico, where he lives with his wife Lynda Schor, the renowned writer and artist, and their magical dog Natasha. His last collection was *Organ Harvest with Entrance of Clones* from Hamilton Stone.

JILL JONES has been published in Australia, UK, USA, New Zealand, Canada, France, Czech Republic and India, and in major anthologies such as *The Penguin Anthology of Australian Poetry*. Her most recent books are *Broken/Open* (Salt, 2005) and *Speak Which* (Meritage Press, 2007).

ADRIANNE KALFOPOULOU is the author of *Wild Greens*, a poetry collection, and *Broken Greek*, a memoir. She has also published two chapbooks, *Fig*, and *Cumulus*. Her second collection of poetry, *Passion Maps*, will be out from Red Hen Press fall 2009. She lives in Athens, Greece.

BHANU KAPIL lives in Colorado. She teaches writing at Naropa University, and Goddard College. Her most recent publication is *humanimal [a project for future children]* (Kelsey Street Press, 2009). She is currently working on a triplicate grid with wet parts, *Schizophrene*.

W. B. KECKLER is the author of *Sanskrit of the Body* (Penguin, 2003). He lives in Harrisburg, Pennysylvania, and blogs at Joe Brainard's Pyjamas. Feel free to stop by for a hot cup of joe.

KARL KEMPTON lives happily with his wife Ruth in Oceano, California consciously removed from literary centers. He conceived and co-founded a poetry festival in San Luis Obispo in 1983; it continues without him. His lexical & visual poems have been widely published and exhibited.

KIT KENNEDY has published in *Blood Orange Review,*
Bombay Gin, CLWN WR, FRiGG, Mannequin Envy,
Runes, Snow Monkey, and forthcoming from *5_Trope,*
Lavanderia, and *Uphook Press.* She hosts the Gallery
Café reading series in San Francisco.
www.authorsden.com/kitkennedy

TRACY KORETSKY'S *Ropeless,* a 15-time
award-winning novel, celebrates possibilities despite
disabilities. Her poetry collection, *Even Before My*
Own Name, is free from www.TracyKoretsky.com along
with links to her widely-published poetry, essays, short
stories and reviews.

GREG KOSMICKI'S recent books are: *We have always been*
coming to this morning (Sandhills Press, 2007) and
Some Hero of the Past (Word Press, 2006). *Marigolds* is
forthcoming from Black Star Press. He is founding
editor and publisher of The Backwaters Press.

GARY LEISING, associate professor of English at Utica
College, has had poems appear in journals including
The Cincinnati Review, River Styx, Sou'wester,
MARGIE, and *Indiana Review.* He was awarded
Indiana Review's 2008 1/2K Award for a prose poem or
short short story.

AMY LEMMON is the author of the collections *Fine*
Motor (Sow's Ear Press, 2008) and *Saint Nobody* (Red
Hen Press, 2009). She holds a PhD in English/Creative
Writing from the University of Cincinnati and is
Associate Professor of English at the Fashion Institute
of Technology.

LYN LIFSHIN has published over 120 books including
three books from *Black Sparrow: Cold Comfort, Before*
it's Light, Another Woman who Looks like Me. Recent
books include *Persephone, Barbaro:Beyond Brokeness,*
Nutley Pond, 92 Rapple, Ruffian. Her web site is
www.LynLifshin.com

DIANE LOCKWARD'S collection, *What Feeds Us* (Wind
Publications), received the 2006 Quentin R. Howard
Poetry Prize. Her poems have appeared in such
journals as *Harvard Review, Spoon River Poetry Review,*
and *Prairie Schooner,* as well as on *Poetry Daily* and
The Writer's Almanac.

RUPERT MALLIN poet, artist and performer based in Norwich. Working mostly visually right now and edits the online mag http://textvisual.wordpress.com/

PAMELA MCCLURE'S first book of poems, *Rock Dove*, was published by Red Dragonfly Press in 2008. She lives in Columbia, Missouri and teaches creative writing and English at Columbia College.

D. H. MELHEM has seven poetry books, three novels, two scholarly books on Black poets, 70+ essays, two anthologies, musical drama. Her novel *Blight* was optioned for film. Recent: *New York Poems; Stigma & The Cave* (SUP). Honors: RAWI Lifetime Achievement; American Book Award, NEH. VP IWWG. www.dhmelhem.com

HILARY MELLON was born in Norwich (UK) in 1949. Her work has been published in over 80 different magazines and anthologies as well as in four pamphlet books. Her first full-length collection *Night With An Old Raincoat* (Headlock 1995) was re-printed in 2000.

PAUL MITCHELL is an Australian poet and fiction writer. His books are *Minorphysics* (IP, 2003), *Awake Despite the Hour* (Five Islands Press, 2007) and *Dodging the Bull* (Wakefield Press, 2007). He is currently completing his first novel. www.paul-mitchell.com.au

CARLEY MOORE'S poetry has been published in *Coconut, Conduit, Fence, Inknode,* and *LIT.* She teaches writing at New York University and is currently working on a young adult novel titled *The Stalker Chronicles.* She lives with her husband and daughter in New York.

DANIEL THOMAS MORAN'S sixth collection of poetry, *Looking for the Uncertain Past,* was published by Poetry Salzburg in 2006. He was poet laureate of Suffolk County, New York from 2005 to 2007. He is Clinical Assistant Professor of Dentistry at Boston University.

MAGGIE MORLEY, editor for the last 10 years of the BAPC's "POETALK," also served as dogsbody for *Blue Unicorn magazine.* Her poems have appeared in publications in the US and UK. Her chapbook *At Blake Gardens* was published in 2005. She also plays tournament Scrabble.

RICHARD NEWMAN is the author of the poetry collections *Domestic Fugues* (Steel Toe Books, 2009) and *Borrowed Towns* (Word Press, 2005). He lives in St. Louis where he edits *River Styx*.

ANGELA ALAIMO O'DONNELL writes poems and teaches English at Fordham University in New York City. She has published two chapbooks, *Mine* (Finishing Line, 2007)and *Waiting for Ecstacy* (Franciscan University Press, 2009). Her collection, *Moving House*, is due out in 2009 (Word Press).

SHIN YU PAI is the author of seven books of poetry, including most recently *Haiku Not Bombs* (Booklyn, 2008), *Sightings* (1913 Press, 2007) and *Works on Paper* (Convivio Bookworks, 2007). For more information, visit http://shinyupai.com.

HELEN PAVLIN has lived in many parts of Australia but for the last ten years, she has made her home in the Northern Territory. Formerly a short story writer, she has recently found the greater compression and intensity of expression offered by poetry to be her medium.

JONATHAN PENTON forged unlikelystories.org in the fires of Mount Doom, and into it poured his hatred, cruelty, and will to dominate.

ALICE PERO is a poet, poetry teacher and musician living in Los Angeles. Her book, *Thawed Stars*, was hailed by Kenneth Koch as having "clarity and surprises." She runs Moonday, the celebrated reading series in Pacific Palisades, CA and has been to Pennsylvania five times.

PATRICK PHILLIPS' first book, *Chattahoochee*, received the 2005 Kate Tufts Discovery Award, and his second, *Boy*, was published in 2008. He has received support from the Fulbright Commission, the NEA, and the Bread Loaf Writers' Conference. He teaches at Drew University.

PAUL PINES is author of *The Tin Angel* (Morrow), *Redemption* (Rocher), and *My Brother's Madness* (Curbstone) and seven books of poetry, *Onion, Hotel Madden Poems, Pines Songs, Breath, Adrift on Blinding Light, Taxidancing* and *Last Call at the Tin Palace*. He lives in Glens Falls, NY.

KEVIN PRUFER'S newest books are *National Anthem* (Four Way Books, 2008) and *Little Paper Sacrifice* (Four Way Books, 2011). He's also editor of *New European Poets* (Graywolf, 2008) and *Pleiades: A Journal of New Writing*. He lives in rural Missouri.

CHELSEA RATHBURN is the author of *The Shifting Line* (U. of Evansville, 2005). Her poems have appeared in *Poetry*, *The Atlantic Monthly*, and other journals. The recipient of a 2009 fellowship in poetry from the National Endowment for the Arts, she lives in Decatur, Georgia.

SUSAN RICH has received awards from the Academy of American Poets, Artist Trust, PEN USA, and the Times Literary Supplement. She is the author of three collections: *The Alchemist's Kitchen, Cures Include Travel* and *The Cartographer's Tongue*. She lives in Seattle, WA.

CYNTHIA NITZ RIS is a freelance editor and teaches composition, creative writing, and law and literature at the University of Cincinnati. Her poetry has appeared in journals such as *Innisfree, Snakeskin*, and *Identity Theory*.

KIM ROBERTS is the author of two books of poems, *The Kimnama* and *The Wishbone Galaxy*. She edits the online journal *Beltway Poetry Quarterly*. Her website: www.kimroberts.org.

JAY ROGOFF'S latest book, *The Long Fault*, appeared in 2008 from LSU Press. LSU will publish his book of dance poems, *The Code of Terpsichore*, in 2011. He has recently completed *Enamel Eyes*, a book-length fantasia on the ballet *Coppélia* and the Franco-Prussian War.

KATE SCHAPIRA writes, teaches, and organizes the Publicly Complex Reading Series in Providence, RI. She's the author of several chapbooks, including *The Love of Freak Millways and Tango Wax* (Cy Gist Press, 2009) and *The Saint's Notebook* (Flying Guillotine Press, 2009).

BARRY SCHWABSKY is an American poet and art critic living in London. He writes regularly for *The Nation* and *Artforum*, among others, and his books include *Opera: Poems 1981-2002* (Meritage Press) and *Book Left Open in the Rain* (Black Square Editions/The Brooklyn Rail).

DEREK SHEFFIELD's collection, *A Revised Account of the West* (2008), won *Flyway's* Hazel Lipa Environmental Chapbook Award. His work has appeared recently in *Poetry, Lyric,* and *Orion*. He teaches at Wenatchee Valley College.

SHOSHAUNA SHY is the founder of Poetry Jumps Off the Shelf as well as BookThatPoet.com, an online resource for poetry event coordinators and poets. Her fourth poetry collection received an Outstanding Achievement Award from the Wisconsin Library Association.

SUE STANFORD is based in Melbourne. Her first book of poetry, *Opal*, appeared in 2006 and her second, *The Neon City*, appeared in 2008. Sue is doing a PhD which includes translating the haiku of some key early 20th century women poets from Japanese.

LUCIEN SUEL Ordinary poet, living in North of France. Translated & published beat poetry in French (Kerouac, Orlovsky, Burroughs, Bukowski, Ginsberg). After lots of poetry books, he's now exploring novel as a new poetical form. *Mort d'un jardinier* (La Table Ronde, 2008).

ROD SUMMERS/VEC, Audio artist/Sound poet. Has published 49 CDs of audio art and sound poetry on VEC AUDIO label which has functioned since 1978. Has performed art and poetry in many Europen countries. See wikipedia for more information.

EILEEN TABIOS' publications include 16 poetry collections, a novel, an art essay collection, a poetry essay/interview anthology, and a short story book. Forthcoming is *The Thorn Rosary: Selected Prose Poems* 1998-2020 (Marsh Hawk Press, 2010).

ELAINE TERRANOVA was a Pew Fellow in the Arts in 2006. Her most recent book is *NOT TO: New and Selected Poems*. She won the Walt Whitman Award for her first book, *The Cult of the Right Hand*. She teaches writing at Community College of Philadelphia and at Rutgers, Camden.

HEATHER THOMAS has seven books of poetry, including *Blue Ruby* (FootHills Publishing, 2008) and *Resurrection Papers* (Chax Press, 2003). Her poems have appeared in more than 30 journals and magazines, and in anthologies including *Common Wealth: Contemporary Poets on Pennsylvania.*

DAVID TIPTON's day job is Assistant Library Director, Spalding University (Louisville). His poems have appeared in *Black Buzzard Review, Recursive Angel, The Louisville Review*, and *Ontologica*. He's at work on the chapbook, *Cloud Movement.*

JUANITA TORRENCE-THOMPSON is Editor/Publisher of *Mobius, The Poetry Magazine* which won best 2007/08 by *Small Magazine Review. Book 5, NY and African Tapestries* was a *Small Press Review* pick. She won the *Writer's Digest* Poetry Award prize 5 of 4,000. She reads, publishes widely in the US & abroad. Columnist.

WILLIAM TROWBRIDGE's poetry collections are *Enter Dark Stranger, O Paradise, Flickers*, and *The Complete Book Of Kong*. His chapbooks are *The Packing House Cantata, The Four Seasons*, and *The Book of Kong.*

PRISCILA UPPAL is a poet, novelist, and professor at York University. Recent works include the Griffin Prize shortlisted *Ontological Necessities* (Exile, 2006) and the novel *To Whom It May Concern* (Doubleday, 2009). *Successful Tragedies* is forthcoming from Bloodaxe books U.K.

KATHRINE VARNES is author of a book of poems, *The Paragon* (Word Tech 2005), and co-editor with Annie Finch of *An Exaltation of Forms* (Michigan UP 2002). Her play, *Listen*, was produced in the summer of 2008. She lives in Larchmont, New York.

JEANNE WAGNER is the author of four collections, including *The Zen Piano-Mover*, winner of the 2004 Stevens Manuscript prize. Another full-length manuscript will be coming out in 2011 from Sixteen Rivers Press. She serves on the editorial staff of the *California Quarterly.*

AMY WATKINS lives in Orlando, Florida, with her husband and daughter. Her poems have recently appeared in *The Louisville Review, Conclave* and *Bayou.* She believes poetry is both lush and stark, comforting and dangerous, complicated and shockingly simple.

SCOTT WATSON was born in 1954 in Philadelphia, PA. He has lived in Japan since 1980. He lives with his wife Morie in Sendai. They have two children. Scott has published over 10 books of poetry plus several translations from Japanese.

MELISSA WEINSTEIN lives in Vermont.

CAROL CLARK WILLIAMS is a retail sales manager who would rather write poetry. At present she is the poet laureate of York, Pennsylvania. She teaches poetry workshops for high school students, senior citizen centers, support groups, and residents of institutions.

JACQUIE WILLIAMS writes poetry and short plays, including *Cyclone Child* a poetry book about Cyclone Tracy. Her daughter was born one week before. Her work has been published in the *Weekend Australian* and other local books.

ERNIE WORMWOOD is a poet and transformative mediator in Leonardtown, Md. She has been published in *Rhino, The Naugatuck River Review,* and in anthologies such as *Poem, Revised,* and *Poetic Voices Without Borders.*

MARK YOUNG's most recent books are *Pelican Dreaming: Poems 1959-2008* (Meritage Press), *Lunch Poems* (Soapbox Press), *More from Series Magritte* (Moria Books) & *terracotta worriers* (ungovernable press). He is the editor of *Otoliths,* and lives in Rockhampton, Australia.

ANDRENA ZAWINSKI, originally from Pittsburgh, lives and teaches writing in Oakland, CA. Her books include *Something About, Traveling in Reflected Light, Greatest Hits, Taking the Road Where It Leads.* Her poetry appears widely in print and online. She is Features Editor at PoetryMagazine.com.

KELLI RUSSELL AGODON "You Ask Why I Write About Death and Poetry" previously published in *32 Poems.* "Kindergarten for Poets" previously published in *PoetLore.*

FLOR AGUILERA GARCIA "The Fair" previously published in *As the Audience Begs for a Ferocious Tango* (San Francisco Bay Press, 2009).

KARREN LALONDE ALIENIER "Stein Writes It All Down" first published in *Looking For Divine Transportation,* The Bunny and the Crocodile Press (DC, 1999). This poem is also part of Alenier's libretto *Gertrude Stein Invents A Jump Early On* that premiered June 15, 2005 by Encompass New Opera Theatre at Symphony Space Leonard Nimoy Thalia in New York City.

SANDRA ALLAND "SASE" previously published in *Taddle Creek Magazine.* "Lost While Translating" previously published in *Proof of a Tongue* (McGilligan Books, 2004).

C. J. ALLEN "The News and the Weather", "The Duck's Back and How it Got Like That", and "Poetry is Your Friend", previously published in *A Strange Arrangement: New and Selected Poems* (Leafe Press, 2007).

ANNETTE BASALYGA "L", previously published in *Verbatim* and *Snakeskin.*

JOHN M. BENNETT "Art of Poetry", previously published in *Meatwatch, Columbus* (Fireweed Press, 1977).

MAXIANNE BERGER "The Other Woman's Poem", previously published in *How We Negotiate* (Empyreal Press, 1999).

F. J. BERGMANN a version of "How to Write Poems # 510", was previously published under the title "Spell" in *espressostories.com.*

GREGORY BETTS a version of "ars poetica: the language of light verse", was previously published in *If Language* (BookThug 2005).

PETER BOYLE "In response to a critic's call for tighter editing" and "Of poetry" previously published in *Museum of Space* (University of Queensland Press, 2004).

ALLEN BRADEN "Medicine Tree" previously published in *Poetry Northwest.* "Revision" previously published in *The Bellingham Review.*

THERESE L. BRODERICK "Ars Poetica" previously published in *Within View.*

NICK CARBÓ "For My Friend Who Complains He Can't Dance and Has a Severe Case of Writer's Block" previously published in *El Grupo McDonald's* (1995).

CATHY CARLISI "Firing Squad or Peanut Butter" previously published in *West Branch.*

WENDY CARLISLE "The Poem Avoids the 'Sincerest Style'" previously published in *Cider Press Review.*

JAMES CERVANTES "In Lieu of an Ars Poetica" previously published in *The Headlong Future* (New Rivers Press, 1990).

JOEL CHACE "no matter" and "wedding" previously published in *Ducky* and *matter no matter* (Paper Kite Press, 2008).

JENNIFER COMPTON "The Pursuit of Poetry" previously published in *Blue* (Ginninderra Press, 2000), and *Poetry.* "Instructions for Open Mic Sessions" previously published in *Parker & Quink* (Ginninderra Press, 2004), and *Quadrant.*

ANNE CORAY "For the Small Poem" previously published in *Ivory* (Anabiosis Press). "Ars Poetica" previously published in *Bone Strings* (Scarlet Tanager Books).

ALISON CROGGON "Ars Poetica" previously published in *The Blue Gate* (Black Pepper Press, Melbourne 1997).

DEL RAY CROSS "Poems" previously published in *Lub Luffly* (Pressed Wafer, 2006).

CRAIG CZURY "White Pall" previously published in *In My Silence to Justify* (FootHills Publishing, 2003). "Uncovering The Mine Shaft" previously published in *God's Shiny Glass Eye* (FootHills Publishing, 2005).

LUCILLE LANG DAY "White Pall" previously published in *Book of Answers* (Finishing Line Press, 2006).

Denise Duhamel "My First Book of Poetry Was Like My First Baby" previously published in *Gargoyle Magazine*.

Riccardo Duranti "The ambush" previously published in *Poems in lieu of an essay on poems*.

Paul Dutton "Content" (hear which syllable you stress) published in *Gam* (2004). "Why I Don't Write Love Poems" and "Missed Haiku" previously collected in *Aurealities* (Coach House Press, Toronto, 1991).

Susanne Dyckman "what to leave" previously published in *equilbrium's form* (Shearsman Books Ltd, 2007).

Lynnell Edwards "Workshop Poem, or Sorry, Austin" previously published in *The Farmer's Daughter* (Red Hen Press, 2003).

Annie Finch "Interpenetrate" previously published in *Calendars* (Tupelo Press, 2003).

Thomas Fink "Nonce Sonnet 4" previously published in *Clarity and Other Poems* (Marsh Hawk Press, 2008).

Alan Halsey "Ars Poetica" previously published in *Not Everything Remotely* (Salt, 2006).

Sharon Harris "Experiment 99a." previously published in *Fun with 'Pataphysics* (Book Thug), and in *AVATAR* (Mercury Press).

Lola Haskins "His Poems" appeared in *Linebreak*. "Epitaph for a Poet" and "Sleep Positions" previously published in *Desire Lines, New and Selected Poems* (BOA Editions, 2004).

Nellie Hill "All Day, Pen Poised" appeared in *Studia Mystica*, 1987 and *Marin Poetry Center Anthology*, 2002.

Paul Hoover "Rehearsal in Black" previously published in *Rehearsal in Black* (Salt Editions, 2001). "Edge and Fold XLI" previously published in *Edge and Fold* (Apogee Press, 2006).

Adrianne Kalfopoulou "Growing" previously published in *Wild Greens*.

Karl Kempton "of ink" previously published by *Light and Dust Books* (USA) and *Word Press* (Japan).

AMY LEMMON "Dislaimer" and "Revival" previously published in *Saint Nobody* (Red Hen Press, 2009).

DIANE LOCKWARD "My Husband Discovers Poetry" previously published in *Eve's Red Dress* (Wind Publications, 2003).

D. H. MELHEM "On the tendency toward solipsism in literature" previously published in *New York Poems* (Syracuse Univ. Press, 2005).

DANIEL THOMAS MORAN "At Hard Labor" previously published in *Poetry Salzburg Review*.

PAUL MITCHELL "Woman Leaves Poetry Seminar" previously published in *fourW*. "Masterclass" previously published in *Cordite*.

RICHARD NEWMAN "Bar Poem" previously published in *Borrowed Towns* (Word Press, 2005).

ANGELA ALAIMO O'DONNELL "A Texas Tale" previously published in *Concho River Review* (Winter 2006).

SHIN YU PAI "Poem" previously published in *Equivalence* (La Alameda, 2003). "A conversation between Huidobro and Braque" previously published in *Gastronomica* (vol. 2, no. 1, February 2002), and *Equivalence* (La Alameda, 2003).

HELEN PAVLIN "Metamorphosis of the Poet" previously published in *Collected Poems* (1993).

JOHNATHAN PENTON "Deep Throat Nihilism" previously published on *kagablog*.

PATRICK PHILLIPS "Ars Poetica: Hitting the Curve" previously published in *Chattahoochee* (The University of Arkansas Press, 2004).

KEVIN PRUFER "There is No Audience for Poetry" previously published in *The Colorado Review* and *National Anthem* (Four Way Books, 2008).

CHELSEA RATHBURN "Teaching Poetry at the School for the Blind" and "Unused Lines" previously published in *The Shifting Line* (University of Evansville Press, 2005).

SUSAN RICH "December Journal Entry" previously published in *5 AM* and *The Alchemist's Kitchen*.

KIM ROBERTS "Mr. Jones Makes Poetry" previously published in *The Amistad* (Spring 2008) and *Fledgling Rag* (Issue 5, September 2007).

JAY ROGOFF "Poets' Park, Mexico DF" and "A Breakdown" previously published in *Southern Poetry Review Vol. 44, No. 2* (2006), and also in *The Long Fault* (Baton Rouge: Louisiana State University Press, 2008).

BARRY SCHWABSKY "On Reverdy Road" previously published in *Shampoo 23* (2005), and *For Despair* (Los Angeles: Seeing Eye Books, 2005).

SHOSHAUNA SHY "White Poem" previously published in *Write Away* from The Rockford Writer's Guild.

SUE STANFORD "Stone Soup" another version of this poem appeared in *Poetry Scotland's Open Mouse*, 2005.

EILEEN TABIOS "Athena" previously published in *Dredging for Atlantis* (Otoliths, 2005).

HEATHER THOMAS "Awakening" previously published in *Ressurection Papers* (Chax Press, 2003).

WILLIAM TROWBRIDGE "New New Formalist" previously published in *Artful Dodge*.

PRISCILA UPPAL "careful careful" previously published in *How to Draw Blood from a Stone* (Exile Editions, 1998). "Sometimes I'm Not Sure I Agree with What I Write" previously published in *Live Coverage* (Exile Editions, 2003).

KATHRINE VARNES "Folding the Laundry I Think About Aesthetics" previously published in *Segue*, issue 1.1.

JEANNE WAGNER "Poems" previously published in *Marin Poetry Anthology*, 2008.

AMY WATKINS "When I Am Asked" previously published in *Halfway Down the Stairs*.

MELISSA WEINSTEIN "Poetics" another version of this poem appeared in *Exquisite Corpse*.

Carol Clark Williams "Chain Poem" previously published in *Grandmother Earth*, Vol. 12, Encore, 1998. "Poetry Lover" previously published in *Byline*, Feb. 2007.

Ernie Wormwood "The Man is Only Half Himself, the Other Half Is His Expression" previously published in *Creation Journal*, 2006.

Mark Young "Keeping my hand in" appeared on the blog *gamma ways*. "untitled" previously published in *Pelican Dreaming: poems 1959-2008*.

Andrena Zawinski "The Poet Driving" previously published in *The Pittsburgh Post Gazette*. "Writing Lesson" previously published in *Paterson Literary Review*, #32.